its discipline and content

literature for children

Pose Lamb
Consulting Editor
Purdue University

Storytelling and Creative Drama—*Dewey W. Chambers, University of the Pacific, Stockton, California*

Illustrations in Children's Books—*Patricia Cianciolo, Michigan State University*

Enrichment Ideas—*Ruth Kearney Carlson, California State College at Hayward*

History and Trends—*Margaret C. Gillespie, Marquette University*

Poetry in the Elementary School—*Virginia Witucke, Purdue University*

Its Discipline and Content—*Bernice Cullinan, New York University*

Children's Literature in the Curriculum—*Mary Montebello, State University of New York at Buffalo*

its
discipline
and
content

BERNICE E. CULLINAN
New York University

Pose Lamb
Consulting Editor
Purdue University

WM. C. BROWN COMPANY PUBLISHERS
Dubuque, Iowa

Printed in the United States of America

Dedicated to my children,
Janie, Jim, and Jonathan Paul

contents

foreword

This series of books came to be because of the editor's conviction that most textbooks about literature for children had not been written for elementary teachers, regardless of the anticipated audience suggested by the titles. The words, *Literature for Children,* preceding each individual title indicate not only the respect for the field held by the authors and the editor but our evaluation of the importance of this type of literature, worthy of consideration along with other categories or classifications of English literature. However, it is *what happens* through books, and the *uses* of literature which are of concern to the authors of this series, as well as the provision of an historical perspective and some knowledge of the writer's and the illustrator's crafts. Our work, then, is directed primarily to the elementary classroom teacher who wants to design and implement an effective program of literature for children.

Because entire books have been devoted to specific topics, for example, the history of literature for children, it is hoped that such topics are covered in greater depth than usual. They are not merely books *about* children's literature; the focus in this series is on helping teachers see what literature for children has been, the direction or directions pointed by scholars in the field, and some ways in which a teacher can share with children the excitement and joy of reading. The authors have tried to share with teachers and prospective teachers their enthusiasm for children's literature, today's and yesterday's; for an unenthusiastic teacher, though well-informed, will not communicate enthusiasm to his pupils.

The author of each book was selected, first because he has demonstrated this enthusiasm in his teaching and writing, and secondly because of his competence in the field of children's literature in general. It is hoped that the thoroughness and depth with which each topic has been

ix

explored and the expertise which each author has brought to a topic in which he has a particular interest will serve as sufficient justifications for such a venture.

Children's literature courses are among the most popular courses in the professional sequence at many colleges and universities. It is rewarding and exciting to re-enter the world of literature for children, to experience again the joy of encountering a new author or of renewing acquaintance with a favorite author or a character created by an author.

The editor and the authors of this series have tried to capture the magic that is literature for children and to provide some help for teachers who want to share that *magic with children.*

Literature can contribute significantly to children's understanding of such recognized curricular areas as science, social studies, mathematics, and English. This is an accepted concept and is neither radical nor innovative.

Less widely accepted, perhaps, and certainly more current, is the proposal made by Dr. Cullinan in this book. She suggests that there is an important place in the curriculum of the elementary school for the study of literature itself. Along with many other serious students of children's literature, she believes that there is a significant body of content related to authors' treatment of plot and characterization, and that there are some important literary genre to which children should be exposed, regardless of the extent to which they relate to current classroom science or social studies projects.

It has been noted that placing emphasis upon the structure of children's literature is not equally acceptable to all who are knowledgeable in the field. There is some concern that overemphasis on structure will inevitably result in overanalysis, and that children will react even less positively to literature than they do now! Indeed, Dr. Cullinan notes that "Just as we would never become acquainted with a person by studying his skeleton, neither should children be introduced to literature by examining its structure." Nevertheless, it cannot be denied that a person's skeleton prescribes some of his more important dimensions. So it is with literature. To guide a child to the point where he can intelligently compare the themes in *The Five Chinese Brothers* and *The Fool of the World and the Flying Machine,* or can contrast the heroes in *Lentil* and *Homer Price* should not and need not result in a less positive response to these books. On the contrary, if the young reader is guided wisely by an adult who *knows* as well as loves much of the literature written for children, both increased understanding and a more positive affective response should result.

The author deals with several seemingly contradictory and competitive approaches to organizing the literature program in the elementary school and makes her own proposals for structuring the study of children's literature. If her suggestions are applied and modified as conditions warrant, parents, librarians, and teachers will almost certainly find their work with children more rewarding, because they will be dealing with an increasingly knowledgeable and more sophisticated audience. Dr. Cullinan raises some very significant questions regarding the sequence of skills and understandings to which children should be exposed. She treats honestly and objectively the major issues involved in the "literary understandings" vs. "appreciation" debate, but it seems quite clear that the author believes that literature for children is an important curricular area, too important to be treated in the casual, haphazard manner to which we've become accustomed.

Pose Lamb, Editor

preface

Elementary school teachers and librarians are accustomed to viewing the field of children's literature as one that contains a wealth of materials with which to enhance the curriculum for elementary school children. Public librarians in children's rooms are forced to recognize the uses of literature in all areas of the curriculum, for they are bombarded with requests for books about space travel, pioneers, and community helpers. The practice of using literature to extend, enrich, and enlarge the curriculum illustrates a utilitarian concept that minimizes literature as an art form. Literature certainly does enrich the total curriculum; however, it would be neglecting a primary value of literature for children if this was where the study of literature stopped.

A curriculum in literature should be built on the body of content and discipline of children's literature. It can be structured in a variety of ways such as, for example, through a study of the divisions of literature, its themes, and forms. What is proposed here is that the structure of the curriculum in literature be determined by the elements of literature itself: the form, the components of plot structure, characterization, setting, theme, and the literary devices. The purpose of this book is not to design a comprehensive curriculum in the discipline and content of literature, for that would require an examination of all literary forms, all components, and all elements of writing style. Rather, the proposals made here are illustrative, not comprehensive, ones for developing a literature curriculum. Since this is a preliminary attempt to construct a literature curriculum based on literary elements, only narrative fiction will be examined.

The approach to literature for children presented in this book is based on the idea that many elements of good literature can be found in works for children. The critic, teacher, parent, or librarian who selects books and guides children to them should themselves recognize basic literary elements and be capable of helping children discover them. Such a literary critic or mentor must know a great deal more about literature than he attempts to teach. For he can rarely lead children to discoveries of literary qualities that he himself has not recognized. Neither can curriculum builders specify content minimums or maximums for groups of children without this information. Therefore, while the major elements of literature and criteria for selection appropriate to a literature curriculum are identified, aspects appropriate for a particular group at a specific age level cannot be specified.

Introducing literature to children through a description of the literary elements apart from the content of literature must be studiously avoided. Just as we would never become acquainted with a person by studying his skeleton, neither should children be introduced to their literature by examining its structure. If, however, they look at the discipline of their literature more closely after they have enjoyed its content or storytelling qualities, then perhaps they can be helped to examine *why* they enjoyed it. Hopefully, they will seek those elements of quality in subsequent literature they read. We cannot start too early to develop critical readers, for the development of complex reading skills requires years of nurturing. But the critical reading of literature is not taught in the same way that the critical reading of informational material is taught. Since literature is the imaginative interpretation of human experience, it must be taught as humanities are taught. It is by recognizing the impact of its form, analyzing its components, and savoring its sensitive comment on the human condition that literature is read critically. Adults who read literature critically can help children grow in their understanding and appreciation of their literature.

Plan of this Book

Familiar and conventional ways of classifying the body of children's literature are useful for many tasks that teachers and librarians perform. The familiar classification systems are less useful in the identification of the elements of quality in literature. The first chapter of this book proposes that the tools of the critic of adult literature be used to identify excellence in children's literature. Subsequent chapters deal with literary form, literary elements, and literary devices or style. A final chapter illustrates discoveries children can make about their literature in the elementary school.

The section on literary form identifies significant features of the forms of narrative fiction. Primary distinctions among forms are discussed, with illustrations of the impact of form on content.

Exploring ways to discern quality of literary elements constitutes a major portion of this book. Plot structure, characterization, theme, and setting are the primary elements through which an author creates an excellent story for children. These elements are, then, the basis for analysis, with some selected passages to illustrate variations of quality.

The discussion of literary style in Chapter 4 explores the manipulation of language for distinguished writing. Elusive qualities of writing style are highlighted in an attempt to discover differences between imaginative work and pedestrian writing.

The final chapter illustrates an approach to literary criticism for elementary school children. Although there are many ways to help children know and appreciate quality in their literature, the approach through shared literary study seems to be a promising one.

I would like to express my appreciation to Elizabeth Wood, Children's Librarian, Port Washington, New York, and Barbara Kleger, doctoral candidate at New York University, for reading and criticizing the manuscript. Prior recognition must go to Charlotte S. Huck, who piqued my interest in children's literature and planted many of the ideas that have come to fruition in this book.

B.E.C.

chapter 1

literary criticism
and children's literature

Parents, teachers, and librarians are empowered with an awesome authority—and commensurate responsibility. They are largely influential in determining the next generation's reading habits, for it is they who screen the crop of books published each year and cull their favorites from previous harvests. They are in the position of helping children select books. The results of their persuasion and the quality of their taste may not be immediately known. But the nature and quantity of adult reading that the children under their guidance will do will ultimately measure their effectiveness.

That children are influenced by the tastes and habits of those around them is rather well-substantiated. Parents' reading habits, the quality of the language used in the home, and the availability of books to a large extent determine the reading habits of the child. Moreover, teachers and librarians also shape children's habits and tastes by making available certain books and by displaying enthusiasm for them. Studies from as early as 1915 support the thesis that children prefer the same books as their teachers do.[1]

More recent evidence confirms the stability of these findings. Cappa[2] found the two most frequent responses to storybooks read aloud were the desire to look at the book and a request to have it retold. Similarly, in another study, books read aloud by teachers were repeatedly chosen for rereading by second graders in low socioeconomic schools.[3] The total literature program did increase the vocabulary and

---

[1]H. J. Wightman, "A Study of Reading Appreciation," *American School Board Journal*, vol. 50 (June, 1915), p. 42.

[2]Dan Cappa, "Kindergarten Children's Spontaneous Responses to Storybooks Read by Teachers," *Journal of Educational Research* (October, 1958), p. 75.

[3]Dorothy Cohen, "The Effect of a Special Program in Literature on the Vocabulary and Reading Achievement of Second Grade Children in Special Service Schools." (Ph.D. diss., New York University, 1966).

reading achievement of the children. Adults do affect children's reading choices, and so they must be prepared to identify and select the best in children's literature.

The elementary school years are a critical period in shaping children's reading tastes. Books read during this period have a lasting effect on lifetime reading habits. Elizabeth Yates poetically contends that "Seeds planted early take deep root."[4] She suggests that very young children have carefully written and illustrated books presented to them, for these contribute to the development of literary taste.

Because early influences matter, the teacher, librarian, and parent must serve as alert critics of children's literature. They can help examine relationships, extend understandings, and enrich meanings in reading that may be unexplored when children are unguided.

Mary K. Eakin assesses the situation aptly:

> Unfortunately children are not born with inherently good taste in their choice of books. Faced with a shelf filled with mediocre titles and one good book, the typical reader, whether a bright, poor, or average student, will read the mediocre books first; he may never even find the one good book. Children do not, of their own accord and with no adult guidance, tend to choose good books in preference to mediocre or poor ones. They will remember the good ones longer and with greater pleasure, but they will not voluntarily choose them without considerable guidance from some adult in whose judgment they have confidence.[5]

Rationale for the Role of the Critic

Some children's literature experts prefer to minimize the guidance of children's reading choices offered by adults. They contend that a child reads primarily for pleasure, and consequently, should make his own selections. This brand of expert supports his argument by saying that he read the Bobbsey Twins and the Hardy Boys without evident harm. The evidence he gives is a *non sequitur* that ignores the possible outcome if only literature of high quality had been read and fails to provide a discernible measure of harm. Fortunately, children now have a large assortment of good books from which to choose. Unfortunately, they also have a large assortment of mediocre books available. If they are not guided in their selection from this literary wealth, they may still become poverty-stricken readers, reading only books of poor quality. Surveys of the amount and quality of reading done by adults reflect

---

[4]Elizabeth Yates. (Lecture, Critical Reading Institute, The Ohio State University, Columbus, Ohio, June, 1963.)

[5]Mary K. Eakin, *Good Books for Children,* 3d ed. (Chicago: University of Chicago Press, 1966), p. x.

negatively upon the guidance they received as children. Current reports of the amount of reading done by elementary school children may indicate an increase in quantity but show little increase in the quality of the books read. In fact, reports available indicate that children's choices differ markedly from adult-selected award books. Rankin found that Newbery Award winners seldom appeared on lists of books most popular with children.[6] Moreover, Norvell's study revealed that children do not give high ratings to books that are rated high by children's literature experts.[7]

When these data are compared with the reports that children prefer the same books their teachers prefer, there is either an anomaly, or teachers are not enthusiastically sharing books of high literary quality with children. Lest teachers be charged with assuming all responsibility, it appears that other significant adults in children's lives do not enthusiastically share and discuss books of high quality with them. It is therefore a proposition, as yet to be proved, that when significant adults know the qualities of good literature and, in turn, are enthusiastic about sharing that knowledge with children, literary tastes will be elevated.

The urgency to acquaint children with high quality literature is intensified by our awareness of competing demands upon their time. The numerous entertainment devices that did not exist even a few decades ago and the greater mobility of the modern child combine to intensify the competition for time. The television set is frequently chosen instead of the book for leisure-time activity. Nila B. Smith reviewed the research on children's televiewing and reading habits, then postulated:

> As compared with reading, data reveal that children on the average are devoting about one hour per day to voluntary reading and three hours per day in viewing television. Perhaps if teachers and researchers were to direct more vigorous effort to the development of keen tastes in and deep appreciations for the content of good books, children would spend less time viewing the bizarre on the screen and more time in communing with the writers of worthwhile literature.[8]

Many parents, teachers, and librarians concerned with the functional reading ability of children have not placed correspondingly high

[6]Marie Rankin, *Children's Interests in Library Books of Fiction,* Contributions to Education, No. 906 (New York: Teachers College, Columbia University, 1944).

[7]George Norvell, *What Boys and Girls Like to Read* (Morristown, N. J.: Silver Burdett Co., 1958).

[8]Nila Banton Smith, "Why Should We Develop Taste in Literature?" in *Development of Taste in Literature,* National Conference on Research in English (Champaign, Ill., National Council of Teachers of English, 1963), p. 5.

priority upon the development of taste in literature. Perhaps the goal, wider reading of higher quality literature, will be more nearly achieved when adults who are significant to the child assume a role of critic.

The critic of children's literature shares his insights and analysis of deeper meanings so that children under his guidance will begin to recognize the qualities of good literature themselves. Matthew Arnold suggested that the function of a critic is to "learn to know and propagate the best."[9] This aptly describes the role of the adult who assumes responsibility for shaping reading habits of a child.

Opponents of the need for reading guidance demand that children be allowed to read for pleasure and not be required to analyze material they choose to read. While allowing that there is a place for reading which is not subjected to analysis, this writer proposes that neither extreme represents the optimum reading pattern for children. Balancing the amount of direction, guidance in analysis, and instruction in critical reading with completely free choice is a preferable route. Assuming that imaginative literature is read primarily for pleasure, which should be the overarching purpose of all instruction in reading of literature, the position stated here implies that appropriately applied skills of analysis can increase understanding of literature and thereby heighten the pleasure obtained.

Necessary and sufficient analysis can increase literary appreciation, but misapplied dissection may vitiate any appreciation that a reader might have had. A sensitive teacher, librarian, or parent realizes when discussion is adequate and maintains a delicate balance. Meckel counters arguments set forth for unguided reading by citing basic principles that are ignored by its proponents.

> It has been assumed customarily that intensive study and analysis have an adverse effect on attitudes and interests, but this assumption obscures certain basic principles: (1) that pupils need literature-reading experiences that develop depth of insight, (2) that unless pupils do considerable reading that is enjoyable, they are not likely to have sufficient practice in reading to develop reading skill or to acquire the habit of reading, and (3) that improvement in literary taste is not likely to develop either in an atmosphere that permits no choice or in a setting that provides no guidance.[10]

To repeat, the major purpose of those who affect children's reading choices must be to build a love for reading and to establish lifetime reading habits in which the search for quality never ends. Guidance

---

[9]Matthew Arnold, "The Function of Criticism," *Lectures and Essays in Criticism* (Ann Arbor: University of Michigan Press, 1962), p. 283.

[10]Henry C. Meckel, "Research on Teaching Composition and Literature," in *Handbook of Research on Teaching*, ed. N. L. Gage (Chicago: Rand McNally & Co., 1963), p. 993. Copyright © 1963 by Rand McNally.

in analysis can raise literary taste which, in turn, should increase pleasure. Rosenheim defines pleasure so that it describes the nature and magnitude of children's happiness. He says the humanistic satisfactions are more than frivolous pleasure:

> Reading to achieve these (humanistic) satisfactions involves, obviously, an energetic act of the intellect—and the capacity for such an act requires cultivation which is certainly not that of mere literacy. It means, to put it bluntly, that we cannot have it two ways: if reading is to yield its deepest, most permanent, most humane satisfactions for our children, then the mere gesture of "reading," mere uncritical pleasure in reading, is not quite enough. If we are concerned with reading for maximum satisfaction, we parents and teachers must be prepared to devise strategies, provide help, and—above all—make judgments about our children's books.[11]

Nor would Rosenheim interpose a watered-down evaluation of literature for children. He insists that the judgment of children's literature be conducted without condescension and without trying to define and enforce values that are uniquely juvenile.[12] Furthermore, he believes the proper satisfactions of reading should provide a robust affirmation of our common humanity, our capacity, whether we are young or old, to understand and to be moved by, and to gather to ourselves the products of the creative imagination. In this spirit, the approach to the study of children's literature described here is proposed; evaluation and analysis should proceed on a basis similar to the evaluation of adult literature.

Analysis and evaluation of adult literature have had long and stormy histories in which various schools of thought prevailed. Frequently, the best seller lists seem to reflect values far removed from literary merit. In a satirical article about the values now prevailing in current adult literature, Marya Mannes quipped:

> Now, happily, due to a mass education designed to produce illiterates, these values [clarity, style, meaning, correct usage of language, and taste] have been discarded not only as meaningless but as indicative of a lack of talent or worse, of vigor. A society, moreover, now gloriously unshackled from the disciplines and restraints that so hampered the da Vincis and Mozarts and Shakespeares has also freed the critic to praise or blame solely on the basis of the two PR's: Popular Relevance and Public Relations.[13]

[11]Edward W. Rosenheim, Jr., "Children's Reading and Adults' Values," in *A Critical Approach to Children's Literature*, ed. Sara Innis Fenwick (Chicago: University of Chicago Press, 1967), p. 7. Copyright © 1967 by the University of Chicago.

[12]Ibid., p. 13.

[13]Marya Mannes, "A Manual for Survival" in Speaking of Books. *The New York Times Book Review*, Section 7, (April 27, 1969), p. 2. Copyright © 1969 by The New York Times Company. Reprinted by permission.

Unfortunately, there are traces of similar practices in the juvenile field; note the spate of children's books about current social problems, books that have little to recommend them other than recency. However, children surrounded with good literature and adults willing to discuss it with them see beyond popular relevance and public relations.

Approaches to the Study of Children's Literature

A field as seemingly amorphous as that of children's literature could yield as many descriptions as there are people examining it. Although the beginning student is not prepared to develop his own category system, he must be shown some form or structure of the field to obtain even a minimal grasp of the content. Among the ways of structuring the content there have emerged approaches that include (1) literary genres or types, (2) motifs, (3) uses of literature, (4) literature for different ages, (5) topical approaches, and (6) classification by literary elements—forms, components, and devices.

Literary Genres or Types. Perhaps the most widely accepted way of looking at children's literature is by its genre or type. This method is seldom a pure taxonomy since it frequently mixes form and content as the basis for the establishment of categories. Thus, the University of Nebraska Curriculum for English describes literature units divided into nine groups which they call pseudo-genres. The Nebraska listing includes folktales, fanciful stories, animal stories, adventure stories, myths, fables, other lands and people, historical fiction, and biographies.[14] The authors state that some of the selections could obviously be placed in more than one group, but they contend that their classification permits stress on certain elements of stories. Stressing particular elements allows the sequential development of principles the authors have identified for the English curriculum. The sequence moves from mythic and anthropomorphic to realistic and analytic literary works.

Huck and Kuhn accept the three major divisions of picture books, prose, and poetry for their category system. Within the category of picture books, both fiction and nonfiction appear. Prose is also divided into fiction and nonfiction, with further specifications within each of these forms as illustrated in the diagram.

---

[14]The Nebraska Curriculum Development Center, *A Curriculum for English* (Lincoln: University of Nebraska Press, 1966), p. ix.

LITERATURE FOR CHILDREN			
Picture Books	**Prose**		**Poetry**
Fiction	Fiction	Nonfiction	Mother Goose
Nonfiction	Realistic — contemporary	Informational	Narrative
	and historical	Biography	Lyrical
	Fantasy		Specialized Forms
	Modern		Haiku
	Traditional — folk and fairy tales		Cinquain
	Fable		Limericks
	Myth		Sonnet
	Legend		

15

Huck and Kuhn's categorization appears to be one of the purest based on form or genre.

May Hill Arbuthnot uses both content and form as she describes the range of stories for children to include picture stories, folktales, stories of family life, historical fiction, biography, animal stories, and fantasy.[16] She does not neglect other forms of literature since she includes the following in the table of contents: Mother Goose and the ballads; poetry; old magic, including folk and fairy tales; fables; myths and epics; new magic, including the modern fanciful tale and space fantasy; animal stories; here and now stories; other times and places; biography; and information books. While this coverage is comprehensive, classifications are made on the basis of both content and form.

Olson and Hedges designed a course to train elementary teachers in the analysis of literature—children's literature and related adult literature. They arranged the sequence of the course in seven divisions paralleling seven kinds of works characteristic of the literature of childhood. These were the parable, the fable, the picaresque, the myth and epic, comedy, poetry, and romance. They recommended that both adult and children's books be examined within each of the seven divisions so that similarities and differences in adult and children's literature can provide a central focus for the course. By comparing similar features in adult and children's literature, the following can occur.

---

[15]Charlotte S. Huck and Doris Young Kuhn, *Children's Literature in the Elementary School*, 2d ed. (New York: Holt, Rinehart & Winston, 1968), p. 655.

[16]May Hill Arbuthnot, *Children and Books*, 3d ed. (Chicago: Scott, Foresman & Co., 1964), p. 19.

The differences can be accounted for in manner and content which separate the excellent and conventional in literature for the child from the excellent and conventional in literature for the adult.[17]

Rosenheim summarized the widely used approaches to the study of children's literature and proposed a change.

For many years, booklists, anthologies, and even literature courses and curriculums tended to classify works according to gross form—poems, plays, and novels—and, within such groups, according to "topic" or "subject matter."[18]

He noted that classification was preceded by judgments about the content of books which were then pigeonholed into some very general category of human experience. This approach is no longer viable, according to Rosenheim, since he believes that there are far more significant categories than the ones previously used. He proposes that some of the categorization be based on the structure and tone of the work and, in particular, the effect that a work has upon the reader. He sees these as far more revealing modes for classification than ones based on content, and he wonders not so much what the reader will learn about as what kind of experience he is invited to undergo.[19] Although he pointed out the shortcomings of the subject matter classifications, he did not attempt to identify the humanistic experiences that might provide appropriate categories.

Northrop Frye's approach to the study of literature puts poetry at the center of all literary training, with literary prose forming the periphery. In his view, there would be no place for training for effective communication or for any form of utilitarian English in a properly constructed literature curriculum. Frye believes that the connections of literature are with the imagination, not with reason; hence, the ideal in literature is one of intensity and power rather than of precision or accuracy. He describes the divisions children should see in narrative fiction.

In any case, all through elementary school a student should become gradually aware that stories come in certain conventional shapes. I think of stories as divisible into four mythoi or generic plots, the romantic, the comic, the tragic and the ironic.[20]

Frye believes the romantic and comic types are appropriate for the elementary school.

[17]Paul A. Olson and Ned S. Hedges, "Analyzing Literature in the Elementary Institute," *Source Book on English Institutes for Elementary Teachers* (Champaign, Ill.: National Council of Teachers of English, 1965), pp. 36-37.
[18]Edward W. Rosenheim, Jr., "Children's Reading and Adults' Values," p. 7.
[19]Ibid., p. 8.
[20]Northrop Frye, "Elementary Teaching and Elemental Scholarship," *PMLA* (May, 1964), pp. 11-18.

Miller examines the relationship between imagination and literature and proposes that the basic concepts of imagination serve as a flexible and spiraling structure of a literature curriculum.[21] He would have children introduced to a large variety of forms and types of literature in the hope that it would help them detect or create an order in their own world. He would acquaint students with duality, perspective, individuality, reality, and feelings through literature. And, finally, he would broaden and deepen their moral awareness, acquaint them with structures and a great variety of forms. Throughout the curriculum, children would be engaged, not only in absorbing, but also in producing; they would be challenged to create a myth or compose a sonnet or write a short story. The composition aspects of Miller's approach parallel those of the Nebraska literature curriculum described above.

Motifs. Several attempts have been made to devise a category system for children's literature, a system that does not depend upon what the story is about. The fundamental, basic characteristics identified as pervasive themes or motifs have been proposed as categories in literature for children. The University of Nebraska Curriculum group identified four structural motifs that cut across the pseudo genres described earlier.[22]

The motifs they identified are related to the sense of family and "other-than-family": (1) a small person's journey from home to isolation away from home; (2) a small person's or a hero's journey from home to a confrontation with a monster; (3) a helpless figure's rescue from a harsh home and the miraculous creation of a secure home; and (4) a conflict between a wise beast and a foolish beast. Motifs are identified when they occur within selections in the various pseudo genres labeled by the Nebraska group.

Rosenheim suggests that the search for basic themes or motifs would help to explain the timeless appeal of certain kinds of stories and poems. He notes that some of man's most basic questions, doubts, and hypothetical answers tend to take form in recurrent literary patterns or archetypes. This kind of search, he believes, brings us closer to identifying the unchanging appeal of certain basic kinds of literary construction.

Awareness of motifs or archetypes, however, suggests that the recognizable to which we respond is not necessarily a matter of times, places, and institutions but of the basic needs we feel, questions we ask, answers we find—of the instinctive, universal challenge of the

[21]James E. Miller, Jr., "Imagination and the Literature Curriculum" in *New Directions in Elementary English,* ed. Alexander Frazier (Champaign, Ill.: National Council of Teachers of English, 1967), pp. 15-34.
[22]Nebraska Curriculum Development Center, *Curriculum for English,* p. xviii.

journey, tension of the conflict, the covert wish that magic mingle with reality, the complex drives of affection, the complex fears of death.[23]

It is his thesis that through literature, children can encounter the human facts of hope and fear, of doubt and reassurance, of need and the fulfillment of need. Rosenheim concludes that it is in encounter with these human facts that we develop uniquely human values, and that these are the values we seek to develop in our children and share with them.[24]

Neumeyer, another critic of the categories into which children's literature has been grouped, points out deficiencies of research studies which report that children like adventure stories better than animal stories. He reviews the development of schema based on motifs, and cites Vladimir Propp's criticism that frequent overlapping occurs in indexing motifs. Neumeyer describes the trend established by Propp, one that he and Alan Dundes, among others, seem to be pursuing.

> In essence, it is maintained by the structuralist critic that there are common denominators within stories. One may look for sequences of action or reaction that, no matter how much the superstructure may vary, remain always the same.[25]

Neumeyer points out that it does not really matter whether the hero is assigned a difficult task by a king or by a genii; it does matter that he is assigned a task. In this way, Neumeyer isolates the functions that particular elements of the story perform. Propp proposes that the functions invariably followed an identical sequence, although in any given story, some functions might be excluded. Neumeyer warns that Propp's functions are not what the English teacher generally calls themes, that his functions are more like verbs than like nouns, and that they are sequences of action and reaction rather than underlying ideas. Neumeyer illustrates how to schematize *Peter Rabbit* according to the Proppian functions:

1. Initial situation. Absence: One of the members of a family is absent from home.
2. Interdiction addressed to the hero.
3. The interdiction is violated.
16. Struggle. The hero and the villain join in direct combat.
22. Rescue. The hero is rescued from pursuit.[26]

Neumeyer proposes that certain structural sequences may appeal to children at certain ages and that only by widespread acceptance of

---

[23]Rosenheim, "Children's Reading and Adults' Values," p. 11.
[24]Ibid., pp. 11-12.
[25]Peter F. Neumeyer, "A Structural Approach to the Study of Literature for Children," *Elementary English,* vol. 44, no. 8, (December, 1967), p. 885.
[26]Ibid.

a common structuring of literature will it be feasible to research such questions.

Uses of Literature. A familiar approach to categorization is one that identifies the educational uses of literature. A proven example of the helpfulness of this approach is Helen Huus's *Children's Books to Enrich the Social Studies.*[27]

A recent extension and refinement of the same approach is found in Cianciolo and LePere's *Literary Time Line in American History.*[28] In these excellent resources for the teacher, the authors identify titles useful in developing and understanding social studies concepts. For instance, if a group were studying a particular event in history, these sources would help them to locate both fiction and nonfiction that add to a knowledge of that period or event. Cianciolo and LePere interspersed dates of historic events and sequenced their annotations according to a time line.

An adaptation of the idea of using books to develop concepts is found in *Reading Ladders for Human Relations.*[29] This publication approaches the area of human relations and values much as the preceding books deal with historical and social studies concepts. Specific titles are identified as being particularly helpful in examining problems of growing up, living with change, and the individual and the group. Literature is examined for the insights it can provide in dealing with personal and social problems. Bibliotherapeutic values are sought in addition to literary value.

Age Groups or Reading Levels. Teachers, librarians, and parents frequently request book lists that are geared to particular age groups or reading ability levels. While these lists generally recognize a two or three grade-level span, there are seldom other bases for division of the books into categories other than reading levels. *I Can Read It Myself*[30] and *Good Reading for Poor Readers*[31] typify this approach to grouping books.

Topical Approaches. A number of bibliographies have been developed around a special topic, an ethnic group, or a subject area. The unifying element varies widely in bibliographies such as *We Build*

---

[27]Helen Huus, *Children's Books to Enrich the Social Studies,* rev. ed. (Washington, D. C.: National Council for the Social Studies, 1966).

[28]Patricia J. Cianciolo and Jean LePere, *The Literary Time Line in American History* (Garden City, N.Y.: Doubleday & Co., 1969).

[29]Muriel Crosby, ed., *Reading Ladders for Human Relations,* 4th ed. (Washington, D. C.: American Council on Education, 1963).

[30]Frieda M. Heller, ed., *I Can Read It Myself* (Columbus: Ohio State University Publications Office, 1965).

[31]George Spache, comp., *Good Reading for Poor Readers,* 4th ed. (Jacksonville: University of Florida, Reading Laboratory and Clinic, 1964).

Together: A Reader's Guide to Negro Life and Literature for Elementary and High School Use[32] and *Growing Up with Science Books.*[33] Each approach to categorization serves a useful purpose for elementary school teachers.

Structural Elements, Form, and Style. The approach to the study of literature proposed in this book is derived basically from aspects of literary criticism. Since it is proposed that the teacher, parent, or librarian serve in the role of critic, study of the field with the tools of literary criticism seems appropriate. The adult who selects literature and acquaints children with it should possess knowledge of criteria, be familiar with the techniques of literary criticism, and serve as a helpful guide while children develop their own literary tastes.

Differing from the preceding examples in that the approach to literature study described herein is not a category system—the analysis of form, elements, and writing style is a means of approaching the field, a means comparable to the critics' approach to adult literature. A study of adult literature should prepare students for the study of children's literature, as well as study in the reverse order. Adults' literature and children's literature provide similar routes to analysis, although differences are observable—in most cases, plots are ordered more sequentially, and characterization is generally less complex in children's books. Despite the distinctions which make specific literary selections more appropriate for children than for adults, the same basic components exist. It is proposed that the study of literature for children proceed by examination of the basic components.

Summary

Research evidence indicates that children prefer the same books that adults significant to them choose to share with them. Adults who influence children's tastes in literature must recognize literary merit and share that which is meritorious with children. Children seldom choose good books of their own accord, with no adult guidance. It is the responsibility of the adults to whom children turn for guidance to recognize quality in children's literature and to develop the beginnings of literary awareness in children.

The field of children's literature is amorphous, and a student of the field needs structure for viewing it. Classification systems have been devised which are based on genre, motifs, uses of literature, reading

---

[32]Charlemae Rollins, ed., *We Build Together: A Reader's Guide to Negro Life and Literature for Elementary and High School Use,* 3d rev. ed. (Champaign, Ill.: National Council of Teachers of English, 1967).

[33]Julius Schwartz, comp., *Growing Up with Science Books* (New York: R. R. Bowker Co., 1966).

levels and age groups, and topical divisions. The approach proposed and developed in this book is based on a study of the literary elements: form, components, and style. The same basic criteria and procedures used for judging adult literature should prove to be useful for judging children's literature. Adults who select literature for and acquaint children with literature need to know the criteria and techniques of literary criticism. Adults who are knowledgeable about literature can guide children toward the development of high literary tastes.

Activities for Further Study

1. Survey the teachers in your school to see how many read aloud to their students. How often do they read aloud? What kinds of books do they read aloud?
2. Record the titles read aloud to an individual child or a group of children over a specified period of time. Analyze the types of books used.
3. Record the choice of books made by children and the choice of books read aloud to them. Compare the lists.
4. Survey a group of children to find out how often they see their parents or other adults in the home reading. Compare this report with the amount of independent reading done by each child.
5. List the books that were significant to you as a child. Recall who helped to make these books available to you.
6. Visit a library story hour. Discuss with the librarian children's favorite books, ones that are read aloud or told.
7. Observe the children who come into the children's room at the public library. Who brings them, who helps them select books? What kinds of problems do they have in finding books?
8. Compare one adult novel with one children's novel. List points that are similar and ones that are different.
9. Survey a group of children to find out who are their favorite characters from children's books. Compare this list to a list of the award book characters.
10. Compare the favorite television programs of children with their favorite books. Are the elements of similarity in satisfactions gained from each? Do they seek similar elements of excitement, fantasy, humor, or sports in their television and literature choices?

Selected References

ARBUTHNOT, MAY HILL. *Children and Books.* 3d ed. Chicago: Scott, Foresman & Co., 1964.

ARNOLD, MATTHEW. "The Function of Criticism." *Lectures and Essays in Criticism.* Ann Arbor: University of Michigan Press, 1962.

CAPPA, DAN. "Kindergarten Children's Spontaneous Responses to Storybooks Read by Teachers." *Journal of Educational Research,* October, 1958, p. 75.

CIANCIOLO, PATRICIA, and LePERE, JEAN. *The Literary Time Line in American History.* Garden City, N.Y.: Doubleday & Co., 1969.

COHEN, DOROTHY. "The Effect of a Special Program in Literature on the Vocabulary and Reading Achievement of Second Grade Children in Special Service Schools." Ph.D. dissertation, New York University, 1966.

CROSBY, MURIEL, ed. *Reading Ladders for Human Relations.* 4th ed. Washington, D. C.: American Council on Education, 1963.

EAKIN ,MARY K. *Good Books for Children.* 3d ed. Chicago: University of Chicago Press, 1966.

FRYE, NORTHROP. "Elementary Teaching and Elemental Scholarship." *PMLA,* May, 1964, pp. 11-18.

HELLER, FRIEDA M., ed. *I Can Read It Myself.* Columbus: Ohio State University Publications Office, 1965.

HUCK, CHARLOTTE, and KUHN, DORIS YOUNG. *Children's Literature in the Elementary School.* 2d ed. New York: Holt, Rinehart & Winston, 1968.

HUUS, HELEN. *Children's Books to Enrich the Social Studies.* rev. ed. Washington, D. C.: National Council for the Social Studies, 1966.

MANNES, MARYA. "A Manual for Survival." *The New York Times Book Review,* April 27, 1969.

MECKEL, HENRY C. "Research on Teaching Composition and Literature." *Handbook of Research on Teaching.* Edited by N. L. Gage. Chicago: Rand McNally & Co., 1963.

MILLER, JAMES E., JR., "Imagination and the Literature Curriculum." *New Directions in Elementary English.* Edited by Alexander Frazier. Champaign, Ill.: National Council of Teachers of English, 1967.

Nebraska Curriculum Development Center. *A Curriculum for English.* Lincoln: University of Nebraska Press, 1966.

NEUMEYER, PETER F. "A Structural Approach to the Study of Literature for Children." *Elementary English,* vol. 44. December, 1967, pp. 883-887.

NORVELL, GEORGE. *What Boys and Girls Like to Read.* Morristown, N. J.: Silver Burdett Co., 1958.

OLSON, PAUL A., and HEDGES, NED S. "Analyzing Literature in the Elementary Institute." *Source Book on English Institutes for Elementary Teachers.* Champaign, Ill.: National Council of Teachers of English, 1965, pp. 35-50.

RANKIN, MARIE. *Children's Interests in Library Books of Fiction.* Contributions to Education, No. 906. New York: Teachers College, Columbia University, 1944.

ROLLINS, CHARLEMAE, ed. *We Build Together: A Reader's Guide to Negro Life and Literature for Elementary and High School Use.* 3d rev. ed. Champaign, Ill.: National Council of Teachers of English, 1967.

ROSENHEIM, EDWARD W., JR. "Children's Reading and Adults' Values." *A Critical Approach to Children's Literature*. Edited by Sara Innis Fenwick. Chicago: University of Chicago Press, 1967.

SCHWARTZ, JULIUS, comp. *Growing Up with Science Books*. New York: R. R. Bowker Co., 1966.

SMITH, NILA BANTON. "Why Should We Develop Taste in Literature?" *Development of Taste in Literature*, National Conference on Research in English. Champaign, Ill.: National Council of Teachers of English, 1963.

SPACHE, GEORGE, comp. *Good Reading for Poor Readers*. 4th ed. Jacksonville: University of Florida, Reading Laboratory and Clinic, 1964.

WIGHTMAN, H. J. "A Study of Reading Appreciation." *American School Board Journal*, Vol. 50, June, 1915, p. 42.

chapter 2

literary forms
of narrative fiction

Authors select a particular literary form for several reasons: it heightens impact, it shapes meaning, and it provides a set of expectations the author can call forth from the reader. The effect of the form on the message was illustrated during the 1969 snow emergency in New York City. Two journalists reported the situation in their editorials on February 14, 1969.

A FABLE OF A GOAT NAMED 'SCAPE'

Once upon a time (this was away back in 1969) there was a goat named 'Scape' who was Mayor of New York City. The other animals kept him around because they had troubles and needed something or other to blame them on, and since 'Scape' was an amiable goat, they naturally blamed everything on him. Now, New York at this time was the double-trouble capital of the animal kingdom. It was overcrowded with animals. It was over-taxed and over-developed and over-anxious, and when it wasn't in a muddle it was in a pickle, and when it wasn't in a pickle, it was in a terrible jam.

"Fun City" the Mayor called it. "Silly goat," replied the animals, but 'Scape' just grinned. When the subways stopped, he took the rap. When the garbage men went on strike, he was the fall guy. When the dockwallopers went fishing, he got all the blame. And when the Negroes and the teachers started a little private war of their own, both took it out on poor old 'Scape'.

. . . .

Then one dreary night it snowed in Fun City. And snowed. AND SNOWED! It came in over the Hudson River and over the Harlem River and the East River in great, billowing white clouds and covered up all the scars, and everything was very beautiful and 'Scape', who was a poetic goat, was very happy.

. . . .

Naturally, none of the animals could get to work and they couldn't even get their newspapers, but instead of being grateful, they berated 'Scape'. They accused him of everything from inventing snow to

16

favoring the rich folk in Manhattan and the black folk in Bedford-Stuyvesant, but he just went out to Queens and listened to the insults and spent three million dollars he didn't have to scrape the snow away.

. . . .

"Why put up with it?" Mary asked. "Why referee a revolution? Why not leave bad enough alone and give Fun City back to Tammany?" But 'Scape' would not listen. "Every goat must have his own identity," he said, "especially in politics, and I'm Mr. Trouble." So he kept going, the handsomest, stubbornest goat in town, scorned by the cops, rebuked by the press, vilified by the Democrats and hated by everybody but the majority of the people. MORAL: NEVER TROUBLE TROUBLE TILL TROUBLE TROUBLES YOU.[1]

Reston used the fable form to heighten the humor and to add meaning to the situation. Another editor used the form of scriptures to describe the same snow emergency.

A Winter's Tale

In the beginning, there was a great storm of snow.
2. And whiteness was on the face of the city. And there arose in the stillness a great lamentation among the people; and it was wondrous loud.
3. And the people lifted up their voices and said, Lindsay, and Moeller, and Eisenbud and Weatherman, why persecute ye us? So sorely were they troubled and beset with confusion and woe.
4. And there came wise men, from the Council of the City and from the Halls of Tammany; and they did each smite the Mayor with the jawbone of an ass, seeking preferment among the populace.
5. And the Mayor rose up and went into the Province of Queens and looked upon the public roads. He thenceforth commanded that more strong men be summoned, to go forth upon the roads with spade and plow. Yet the people were exceeding wroth and said unto the Mayor, Begone, wretched man.
6. And in the Province of Manhattan, there rose a great whirlwind among the leaders of the Legions of DeLury, who cried, The city walloweth in filth.
7. But the leader of the Legion harkened not back unto the days when the streets overflowed because the Legion was idle.
8. And there came others who said, with righteousness, it was not thus in the Proconsulship of Wagner. Let the Mayor and Moeller and Eisenbud and Weatherman account to us for their misdeeds. And the Mayor responded, Let Weatherman answer for it. Nor was there an end to recrimination.
9. And in this wise, they disputed. But the little children of the city gamboled in the snow and there were among their elders those who

[1]James Reston, editorial, *The New York Times*, February 14, 1969, p. 38. Copyright © 1969 by The New York Times Company. Reprinted by permission.

counselled, Let us not judge wrathfully or in haste but seek out how
we may act prudently henceforward for the snow falleth on the just
and the unjust alike.[2]

The effect of literary form on the content is illustrated in children's
literature in stories about Paul Revere and Paul Bunyan. By casting
Paul Revere's story in verse with the rhythm of hoofbeats, Longfellow
emblazoned his version of events on the minds of children. Facts cited
in Longfellow's poem are remembered far more widely than those he
ignored.[3] Similarly, Ennis Rees's use of form adds an intriguing dimension to Paul Bunyan's story in *The Song of Paul Bunyan and Tony
Beaver*.

> And Paul found that it was especially hard
> To give the men all the flapjacks they wanted.
> This problem grew worse when Babe the Blue Ox
> Developed a craving for hot cakes and honey
> As fierce as that of the men themselves—
> If not, in fact, fiercer, for Sourdough Sam
> Would no sooner pour the first big flapjack
> On top of his special flapjack stove
> Than the delicate fragrance would wake Babe up,
> And there he would be with his head through the window
> Gobbling up every flapjack in sight.[4]

It becomes evident, then, that authors manipulate form as well as
content to achieve desired meaning.

Literary form is the shape or model a work assumes as a result of
the technical and artistic resources used by the author. Most forms of
narrative fiction developed from a tradition of oral literature although
additional forms have been created by modern authors. Form needs to
be examined in its relationship to content, since form functions to mold
content into a highly complex organization. Identifiable characteristics
plus an accepted set of conventions have become so associated with
each literary form that authors now consciously employ them to achieve
a desired effect. And, conversely, the reader correspondingly sets his
expectations according to certain recognized forms. Georgiou sees genre
groupings as an outgrowth of synthesis of form and idea in literature.

> The synthesis of discovery and creation, or the interrelatedness of
> the idea and its treatment has been a focus of the literary artist and

---

[2]Editorial in *New York Post*, February 14, 1969, p. 48. Reprinted by permission
of New York Post. Copyright © 1969, New York Post Corporation.

[3]Henry Wadsworth Longfellow, *Paul Revere's Ride*, illustrated by Paul Galdone. (New York: Thomas Y. Crowell Co., 1963).

[4]Ennis Rees, *The Song of Paul Bunyan and Tony Beaver*, illustrated by Robert
Osborn. (New York: Pantheon Books, a division of Random House, Inc., 1964),
p. 36.

critic in most eras. An outcome has been classification of genre conceptions or groupings of literary types.[5]

Despite the fact that genre conceptions and literary types are now rather clearly defined, critics must be alert to mixed forms that abound. Frye points out that the forms of prose fiction are mixed, like racial strains in human beings, not separable like the sexes.[6]

Mixing forms and generating new ones provide the creative author vehicles through which he can execute his art. Wellek and Warren insist that a good writer partly conforms to the genre as it exists, and partly stretches it.[7] That is, he draws upon the aesthetic devices related to form, devices that are already intelligible to the reader, and sometimes he improvises with them.

Need for Identifying Form

Critics of adult and children's literature should readily recognize the conventions associated with each literary form. Danziger and Johnson justify this need.

> Important as it is to analyze a novel, play, or poem in and for itself, it is often just as important to know to what group or family it belongs. We are interested in such classification not just for the sake of tidiness, but rather because it is helpful to know the background, the traditions or conventions a writer is either using or consciously playing against. We may, in fact, limit or actually distort the meaning of a work if we ignore its literary background.[8]

Indeed, for two salient reasons, it is useful for the student of children's literature to identify acknowledged literary forms. First, form provides a structure for viewing the field of children's literature and aligns it with the categories of universal literature. Second, determining form, as noted above, is a basic step for critical analysis. Elizabeth Nesbitt underscores this necessity for critics of children's literature to recognize literary form.

> Since these books show great variety of kind, critics should be able to define clearly the requirements of each form of literature and to

---

[5]Constantine Georgiou, *Children and Their Literature* (Englewood Cliffs, N. J.: Prentice-Hall, 1969), p. 47. Copyright © 1969. Reprinted with permission of Prentice-Hall, Inc.

[6]Northrop Frye, *Anatomy of Criticism* (Princeton, N. J.: Princeton University Press, 1957), p. 305.

[7]René Wellek and Austin Warren, *Theory of Literature*, 3d ed. (New York: Harcourt, Brace & World, 1956), p. 235.

[8]Marlies K. Danziger and W. Stacy Johnson, *An Introduction to Literary Criticism* (Lexington, Mass.: D. C. Heath & Co., 1961), p. 64. Copyright © 1961 by D. C. Heath & Co., Lexington, Mass.

establish with equal clarity whether or not the book in question lives up to these requirements.[9]

It seems patent, therefore, with regard to form, that knowledge of its conventions, recognition of its uses, and sensitivity to its nuances are prerequisites for critical analysis. Because each form has recurrent features which the reader may anticipate, the characteristics provide a structure for criticizing an individual selection. Viewing a work of narrative fiction as a unity and in relation to other works of the same genre contributes to a more valid assessment. Nesbitt distinguishes purposes of critical assessment in this way:

> A competent critic does not approach the critical reading of a book with the preconceived intention of finding in it things that may be destructively criticized, with the hope that on page so-and-so he may find language, incidents, details, attitudes to which he may object, thereby proving to himself, and hopefully only to himself, that he is critical. So he is, but in the petty, carping sense of the word.

Rather, she continues:

> The competent critic, when he does find something deserving of adverse criticism, does not draw it completely out of context, thereby exaggerating it out of proportion. Also, if he is competent, he has a sense of the fitness of things, a realization that the true test of style is fitness of form and expression to thought and nature of content.

She aptly concludes:

> It is one thing to analyze and dissect a book, so that at last it lies in disjointed, heterogeneous fragments. It is another thing to rebuild from these fragments the whole of a book; to paraphrase Stevenson, it is another thing to give a book body and blood. But it is essential that any critical comment leave the reader or listener with a totality of impression, because otherwise less than justice has been done to a book, even to those that may miss greatness.[10]

Traditional and Modern Literary Forms

Categorizing all narrative prose by form is fraught with the dangers of oversimplifying, of imposing rigidity upon forms, and of identifying only skeletal features of literature. Despite the dangers, rational structuring can help a critic who is developing and organizing his knowledge in a new area. Traditional forms are representative of the ways man has commented about himself and his condition through the ages. It

---

[9]Elizabeth Nesbitt, "The Critic and Children's Literature," in A *Critical Approach to Children's Literature*, ed. Sara Innis Fenwick (Chicago: University of Chicago Press, 1967), p. 124. Copyright © 1967 by the University of Chicago.
[10]Ibid., pp. 124-125.

includes forms that had their origin in primitive ritual and ones used for cultural indoctrination through the centuries. Modern forms of literature have grown out of the traditional literature and out of man's need to express himself creatively. Despite the intermingling of forms, most narratives for children can be grouped under either traditional or modern labels.

TRADITIONAL FORMS

A major part of children's literary heritage appears in certain conventional forms which grew from an oral tradition and was used to instruct, to entertain, and to solidify communities of people. Parables taught lessons, fables had direct and pointed morals, and folktales illustrated traits valued by a culture. Perhaps due to the oral transmission, traditional forms have strong rhythmic language patterns and many repetitive devices. These stories are attributed to no single author, since many generations of people shaped their present form. Traditional literature encompasses parables, fables, folktales, fairy tales, myths, and legends among the narrative forms. Wellek and Warren call these primitive forms.[11]

Parables. Parables tell a brief story from which a moral or a spiritual truth can be inferred. Olson and Hedges describe parables as

> . . . works in which human or human-like exemplars of symbolic actions cluster about a single symbolic object or a group of objects and give a kind of luminousness to a cultural or religious ideal; a sower sowing grain, a prince storing grain for survival, two men building houses, three pigs building houses, two trees standing side by side, two girls giving water to an old lady at a well, an old man carving a stick—these are the matter of children's stories and of profound teaching.[12]

Similar to the fable in that action revolves around a symbolic object or idea, the parable differs in that the things symbolized are represented by human characters. Human characters exemplify the composite qualities needed to illustrate the spiritual lesson in the parable, whereas they are usually represented by animals in a fable. The Prodigal Son, the Good Samaritan, the Wise and Foolish Virgins, and other parables use human characters to represent respectively the abstractions of a father's love, caring for others, and vigilance. Recent attempts to include Biblical literature in elementary school curricula have created

---

[11]Wellek and Warren, *Theory of Literature,* p. 234.
[12]Paul A. Olson and Ned S. Hedges, "Analyzing Literature in the Elementary Institute" in *Source Book on English Institutes for Elementary Teachers* (Champaign, Ill.: National Council of Teachers of English, 1965), p. 39.

a demand for publication of parables individually bound and illustrated. Two such parables are *The House on the Rock*[13] and *Jon and the Little Lost Lamb.*[14]

Inclusion of Biblical literature in a curriculum for children seems justified by research that cites high frequency of allusions in adult life and literature that are derived from Biblical sources. Acknowledgment and use of the parable form as a part of children's literary heritage, for example, does not imply using parables to teach moral and ethical precepts. The parable should be identified as a traditional form of literature which demonstrated man's belief in universal truths, a form that provides an interesting commentary on human strengths and frailties.

Fables. Fables are simple, highly condensed lessons in morality. They are brief narratives intended to illustrate an abstract idea of good or bad, wise or foolish behavior in a concrete and dramatic form so that it is remembered. The characters are generally animals, but some are inanimate objects that represent man; they engage in a single significant act which teaches a moral lesson. Characters are not developed or given any dimension other than the virtue or folly they portray, for they are used as symbols. The clever fox is the epitome of cunningness; he is that characteristic personified. The moral is obvious and is stated explicitly; virtues of prudence, moderation, humility, and forethought are often stressed. The fable form resembles the parable, but differs insofar as fables include improbable and impossible happenings. Hollowell distinguishes between the parable and the fable in her statement, "The parable may be said to be a story true to facts, while the fable is principally true to the truth presented."[15]

Fables derived from an oral tradition but have served as a writing model for modern authors. Marcia Brown's fable from India, *Once a Mouse,*[16] Barbara Cooney's *Chanticleer and the Fox,*[17] and Leo Lionni's *Tico and the Golden Wings*[18] are three modern examples.

Many of the traditional fables have been adapted or illustrated in single editions. Brian Wildsmith illustrated some French fables, such as

---

[13]Jane Latourette, *The House on the Rock,* illustrated by Sally Matthews (St. Louis, Mo.: Concordia Publishing House, 1966).

[14]Jane Latourette, *Jon and the Little Lost Lamb,* illustrated by Betty Wind (St. Louis, Mo.: Concordia Publishing House, 1965).

[15]Lillian Hollowell, *A Book of Children's Literature,* 3d ed. (New York: Holt, Rinehart & Winston, 1966), p. 99.

[16]Marcia Brown, *Once a Mouse . . . A Fable Cut in Wood* (New York: Charles Scribner's Sons, 1961).

[17]Barbara Cooney, adapter, *Chanticleer and the Fox,* illustrated by Barbara Cooney (New York: Thomas Y. Crowell Co., 1958).

[18]Leo Lionni, *Tico and the Golden Wings,* (New York: Pantheon Books, 1964).

The Lion and the Rat[19] and *The Rich Man and the Shoemaker*.[20] The well-known Greek fables are found in the collection, *Aesop's Fables*,[21] by Louis Untermeyer and again in *Fables of Aesop*,[22] retold by James Reeves. Indian Jataka tales and *The Fables of Bidpai* are further sources for study of the traditional fable form.

Folktales. The term folktales, a part of folklore, encompasses all literary heritage from the oral tradition. Thompson broadens the category to include all forms of the narrative, both written and oral, that have been handed down through the years.[23] In this sense, the category includes all folklore, such as songs, ballads, chants, dance rituals, fairy tales, fables, myths, legends, and epics. Arbuthnot identifies folktale as a variety of folklore:

> Folklore is sometimes called the "mirror of a people." It reveals their characteristic efforts to explain and deal with the strange phenomena of nature; to understand and interpret the ways of human beings with each other; and to give expression to deep, universal emotions —joy, grief, fear, jealousy, wonder, triumph. Of the many varieties of folklore, the folktale is the most familiar and perhaps the most appealing.[24]

The folktale, then, as one variety of folklore, does reflect the language and values of the culture from which it grew. Anthropologists profitably use the literature of a culture to study its mores. Arbuthnot summarizes the conclusion of many social anthropologists:

> . . . folktales have been the *cement of society*. They have not only expressed but codified and reinforced the way people thought, felt, believed, and behaved. Folktales taught children and reminded their elders of what was proper and moral. They put the stamp of approval upon certain values held by the group, and thus cemented it together with a common code of behavior.[25]

Thus, the recurrent themes of rewarding cleverness and hard work, of goodness overcoming evil and greed are expressions of the traits that

---

[19]La Fontaine, Jean de, *The Lion and the Rat*, illustrated by Brian Wildsmith (New York: Franklin Watts, 1964).

[20]La Fontaine, Jean de, *The Rich Man and the Shoemaker*, illustrated by Brian Wildsmith (New York: Franklin Watts, 1965).

[21]Louis Untermeyer, selector and adapter, *Aesop's Fables*, illustrated by A. and M. Provensen (New York: Golden Books, 1965).

[22]James Reeves, ed., *Fables of Aesop*, illustrated by Maurice Wilson (New York: Henry Z. Walck, 1962).

[23]Stith Thompson, *The Folktale* (New York: Holt, Rinehart & Winston, 1951), p. 4.

[24]May Hill Arbuthnot, *Children and Books*, 3d ed. (Chicago: Scott, Foresman & Co., 1964), p. 252.

[25]Ibid., p. 255.

a group of people sought to have their young emulate. The purpose of the folktale seems to be similar to that of the parable and fable, since it was an attempt to teach some precept while it entertained. Many folktales tell of people making the best of a situation and illustrate how courage and humility win out. Other folktales are more closely allied with the myth insofar as their purpose was to explain human and animal characteristics or social customs.

The folktale form is readily identified by its recurring features. Some of the characteristics are undoubtedly due to the oral tradition, namely, the repetition of events and language patterns. The repetitive language and action provided a frame-work to aid the storyteller's memory. Other stylistic features include simplicity of incident, lack of specificity of time and place, and a summary of action in a sentence or two. The three little pigs, the three brothers, and the three Billy Goats Gruff go out to encounter three incidents. Each character and each incident involves the repetition of some language pattern and a rhythmic response.

Characterization is generally limited in the folktale because characters are used to symbolize wise or foolish behavior, total goodness or evil. It is similar to the fairy tale in this respect, although the forms differ insofar as the characters of folktales are usually common folk engaged in common activities. The folktales tell of soldiers making soup, women with eggs and sausages, or pigs and chickens; whereas the fairy tales characteristically deal with kings and queens, princes and princesses.

The traditional folktale form is used by modern authors. For example, in *The Rain Puddle*,[26] Holl tells of a plump hen who is concerned that another plump hen has fallen into a rain puddle. As she spreads the word in true Chicken Little fashion, each of the other barnyard animals runs to look, and each sees one of his kind in the puddle. The catastrophic situation ends when the rain puddle dries up.

Fairy Tales. Fairy tales are properly a part of traditional folk literature; specifically, they are stories dealing with magic and the supernatural, and featuring fairies, giants, dwarfs, and royalty. Traditional fairy tales have no known author but were collected and written down by a number of men, including Charles Perrault, Jacob and Wilhelm Grimm, Peter Asbjörnsen and Jörgen Moe. A recent statement clarifies the relationship of the fairy tale to other folk literature.

> Fairy tales are one class of the genus folktales. All sorts of traditional narratives fall under the general heading "folktales," but of these,

---

[26]Adelaide Holl, *The Rain Puddle*, illustrated by Roger Duvoisin (New York: Lothrop, Lee & Shepard Co., 1965).

fairy tales are those laid in a world of wonders and marvels. They are distinct from ghost stories, legends, myths, and various other kinds of folktales (all of which may have some elements of the supernatural or motifs involving magic) in that they are totally concerned with imaginative wonders; they are woven whole-cloth out of fantasy.[27]

Fairy tales are similar to other traditional literature in the development of characterization; their characters are flat, for they are symbolic and represent total goodness or total evil. O'Neill-Barna continues with the distinguishing features of the fairy tale.

In a fairy tale, the art of telling is all. The plot is the least characteristic element since all fairy tale plots are very much like each other in their simple structure and invariable sequences of action (prohibition-violation, persecution-deliverance, search-reward) independent of who performs them. What makes a fairy tale great is its style—its economy of language, vivid details, turns of speech—and these were up to the teller, the active bearer of tradition. He could choose from and improve upon all the versions known to him from generations of storytellers who had chosen and improved before him. Since his audience, the passive bearers of tradition, would also approve or disapprove and see that the tale kept to its tracks, this was a mutual process and what was retained was fine indeed.[28]

In fact, the language of the fairy tale contributes so much to its beauty that simplified versions are totally unjust. Phrases, such as "There was once a very learned man in the north-country who knew all the languages under the sun, and who was acquainted with all the mysteries of creation,"[29] lose some of their majesty when shortened or simplified.

The structure of the fairy tale is simple; there is a straightforward plot line, a section that introduces the flat characters and a conflict, the development of the problem, and a conclusion or resolution. It is the use of interesting language that makes it possible to contain a story within this simple framework. The language, too, helps to create an indefinite sense of time and place. Introductory phrases, such as "once upon a time," "long ago and far away," "there was once a shoemaker," and "long, long ago there lived an old man and an old woman," add to the feeling of all times, all places. The collections cited in the bibliography illustrate the variety found in folk and fairy tale.

---

[27]Anne O'Neill-Barna, "All in the Telling," *The New York Times Book Review*, Section 7, Part II, (November 9, 1969), p. 3. Copyright © 1969 by The New York Times Company. Reprinted by permission.

[28]Ibid. Copyright © 1969 by The New York Times Company. Reprinted by permission.

[29]Joseph Jacobs, collector, "The Master and His Pupil." *English Fairy Tales*, illustrated by John D. Batten (New York: Dover Publications, 1898, 1967), p. 73.

Myths. Myths are a part of traditional literature and folklore. They are complex and symbolic explanations of man's existence. Primitive peoples used myths to explain events in nature, to describe relationships between men and the supernatural, and to explain the origins of human civilization. In referring to myth, Huck and Kuhn say

> . . . it evolved as primitive man searched his imagination and related events to forces as he sought explanation of the earth, sky, and human behavior. These explanations moved slowly through the stages of a concept of one power or force in human form who controlled the phenomena of nature; to a complex system in which the god or goddess represented such virtues as wisdom, purity, or love; to a worshipping of the gods in organized fashion. Gods took the form of man, but they were immortal and possessed supernatural powers.
>
> Myths deal with men's relationships with their gods, with the relationship of the gods among themselves, with the way men accept or fulfill their destiny, and with the struggle of man between good and evil forces both within and without himself.[30]

Through myths, primitive people personified the mystical forces in the universe; they could explain the movements of the sun, the sea, and the moon with myths when they had no scientific explanations. Myths were an attempt to interpret facts and were accepted as truth by the people who heard them. A study of the Greek, Roman, or Norse culture is incomplete without an examination of the myths from each culture. Asimov's *Words from the Myths*[31] provides ample evidence of the need to include mythology in the study of children's literature.

Legends. Myths and legends are so closely related that many literature scholars combine them into one group. There are distinctions between them; whereas myths were pure fantasy made up as explanations of natural phenomena, legends are based on a grain of truth. Frequently, the slight historical fact has been so distorted and magnified that it is hardly recognizable in the legend. Many legends are etioliogical; they demonstrate the reasons for customs; they propagandize national or religious ideals. Legends have been called the idealization of history. Frequently called hero tales, they characteristically present a strong male figure with whom the citizenry can identify. The central male characters, who become larger than men, symbolize power, perform good deeds, and accomplish significant goals for the national group.

Legendary heroes have particular appeal for intermediate grade boys. Pyle's retelling of *Some Merry Adventures of Robin Hood, of*

---

[30]Charlotte Huck and Doris Young Kuhn, *Children's Literature in the Elementary School,* 2d ed. (New York: Holt, Rinehart & Winston, 1968), pp. 192-193.
[31]Isaac Asimov, *Words from the Myths,* illustrated by William Barss (Boston: Houghton Mifflin Co., 1961).

Great Renown in Nottinghamshire[32] provides the daring, intrigue, and adventure that captures these readers' interest.

Toor's collection of folktales, fairy tales, and legends of Italy, Greece, and Sicily gives the reader a flavor of the cultural values from those countries.[33]

James Houston's *Tikta'liktak: An Eskimo Legend*[34] recounts the story of a young Eskimo hunter who was carried out to sea on an ice floe. His behavior exemplifies the virtues admired by the stoic Eskimos.

MODERN FORMS

The most prevalently used form of narrative fiction for children is the novel. Children's novels usually represent more complexity than is found in more traditional forms of literature. In the novel, characters are more fully developed, plots are more complicated, and settings are more fully described. Depending upon the level of sophistication of the critic, many perspectives for study of children's novels are available. Certain basic similarities in the structural elements of children's and adults' fiction suggest that forms of fiction identified in adult novels may have qualified applicability for children's novels. Northrop Frye distinguishes among four forms of narrative fiction: the novel, the romance, the Menippean satire or anatomy, and the confession.[35] He submits that when these forms are mistakenly lumped together, distorted analyses result. Frye believes accurate identification of form is important so that a work can be examined in terms of the conventions the author chose.

The distinction between the novel and the romance is primarily in the conceptualization of character. The novelist presents realistic characters; the romancer presents stylized figures who expand into psychological archetypes. Frye describes the confession as intellectual and introverted in form, centering on thought that is neither quite religion nor philosophy. Anatomy, or Menippean satire, is concerned less with people than with mental attitudes and, since the individuals in the satires are really mouthpieces for the ideas they represent, characterization is stylized. Frye describes the anatomy form as presenting a vision of the world in terms of a single intellectual pattern. He suggests that *Alice in Wonderland* and *The Water Babies* are perfect Menippean

---

[32]Howard Pyle, *Some Merry Adventures of Robin Hood, of Great Renown in Nottinghamshire* (New York: Charles Scribner's Sons, 1954).

[33]Frances Toor, *The Golden Carnation; and Other Stories Told in Italy,* illustrated by Anne Marie Jauss (New York: Lothrop, Lee & Shepard Co., 1961).

[34]James Houston, *Tikta'liktak: An Eskimo Legend* (New York: Harcourt, Brace & World, 1965).

[35]Frye, *Anatomy of Criticism.*

satires, and, according to his criteria, so are *James and the Giant Peach*[36] and *Charlie and the Chocolate Factory*.[37]

In Frye's terms, then, most realistic fiction for children would qualify as novels, while fantasies would more probably approximate romances. Although some children's books are not easily fitted into Frye's categories, use of his distinctions does suggest more precise evaluations. The more widely used terms of realism and fantasy, however, currently serve to classify modern forms of children's literature. Realism is distinguished from fantasy by a judgment as to whether or not the story could occur in the real world. But their mode of characterization is, perhaps, a valid discriminator. Certainly, in this vein, Frye's parallels of novel and romance would seem defensible. These features are distinguished further in the next sections.

Modern forms of narrative fiction, then, are those works directed toward some aesthetic purpose, having a developed body of content and attributable authorship. Although the major forms are the realistic and the fanciful novel, modern authors use the primitive forms intentionally to achieve a particular effect, such as Thurber's use of the fable form in *Fables for Our Time*,[38] and the fairy tale form in *Many Moons*.[39] The picture storybook depends heavily upon the graphic elements to communicate, in addition to its narrative, but even so, it may still be classified as realism or fantasy.

Fantasy. Fantasy is the label used for literature that brings magic and impossible happenings into the realm of the plausible for children. Growing from the fairy tale tradition with its feats of supernatural powers, enchantments, little people, time manipulations, giants and talking beasts, modern fantasies build similar elements into a more fully developed form. Characters in modern fantasies are not symbolic as they are in traditional forms, and yet they are still stylized. These characters engage in a well-structured plot, and their action in it relays a meaningful theme. Generally, fantasies begin in a realistic setting and move gradually into the world developed in the fantasy. Many fantasies are similar to Frye's definition of the romance, while others are satires. Some of the satirical stories provide a commentary on society and the individual versus the group struggle. Kendall's *The Gammage Cup*[40] satirizes social customs and values by telling of five villagers

---

[36]Roald Dahl, *James and the Giant Peach*, illustrated by Nancy Ekholm Burkert (New York: Alfred A. Knopf, 1961).

[37]Roald Dahl, *Charlie and the Chocolate Factory*, illustrated by Joseph Schindelman (New York: Alfred A. Knopf, 1964).

[38]James Thurber, *Fables for Our Time*, (New York: Harper & Row, 1940).

[39]James Thurber, *Many Moons*, illustrated by Louis Slobodkin (New York: Harcourt, Brace & World, 1944).

[40]Carol Kendall, *The Gammage Cup*, illustrated by Erik Blegvad (New York: Harcourt, Brace & World, 1959).

who are forced to leave their Minnipin village because they do not conform to the town behavior code. Muggles and her friends refuse to paint their front doors green and to wear green sashes as demanded by the village powers. Because of their nonconformity, they are forced to leave but are welcomed back as heroes after they save the village from destruction.

The classic *The Wind in the Willows*[41] illuminates the nature of mankind through Grahame's descriptions of life along the river bank. The friendships of Water Rat, Mole, Badger, and the pompous Toad represent more than is revealed through surface level reading. The stoats and the weasels and each of the central characters represent more than his literal self. Similarly, the virtues and values found in *Charlotte's Web*[42] portray in action some of the noblest relationships found among human beings.

The fantasy form is uniquely suited and used for the technique of revealing human nature by casting the truth into dimensions the reader can accept. The bulk of fantasy, however, is not a commentary on the human condition, but is imaginative play which delights and entertains children of all ages.

Realism. Realistic fiction portrays life as it could possibly happen in the physical world. The setting may be either contemporary or historical, but the characters are realistic, and they behave as normal human beings without magical powers. Realistic fiction includes animal stories in which the animals behave as natural animals, humorous stories, adventure stories, and all other stories in which realistic behavior is maintained. The characters, plot action, and setting must all remain within the realm of the possible.

A work is not judged as being realistic by its verisimilitude in detail to a physical place but, rather, by the illusion of reality created within the world of that book. Realistic fiction is an attempt to present a believable slice of life, but the incidents are selected and shaped to suit the author's aesthetic purpose. Poetic license allows the author of realistic fiction to cover a year in one sentence and to spend an entire chapter on one hour if that sense of timing suits his purpose. In fact, children would not continue to read literature that progressed at the same pace as their own lives, and so authors alternate summary and scene advisedly. Because routine tasks pale quickly, the wise selection and arrangement of incidents is a necessary storytelling skill.

---

[41]Kenneth Grahame, *The Wind in the Willows,* illustrated by E. H. Shepard (New York: Charles Scribner's Sons, 1908, 1953).
[42]E. B. White, *Charlotte's Web,* illustrated by Garth Williams (New York: Harper & Row, 1952).

Characterization in realistic narratives for children tends to be natural, with only central characters being fully developed. The hero is presented in many dimensions so that the reader will care about what happens to him.

The following books illustrating the broad scope of realism are suggested for study: contemporary life, *From the Mixed-Up Files of Mrs. Basil E. Frankweiler*;[43] historical times, *Johnny Tremain*;[44] animals, *King of the Wind*;[45] humor, *Henry Reed's Babysitting Service*;[46] minority groups, *South Town*;[47] mysteries, *The Egypt Game*;[48] and other lands, *North to Freedom*.[49] Further subdivisions, such as sports stories, war stories, and fictionalized biography, demonstrate the comprehensive nature of the realism category.

Summary

Authors express their ideas in a particular literary form intended to achieve a desired aesthetic purpose. Literary forms are recognizable models of prose which have identifiable conventions to which authors conform, but occasionally expand. The characteristics of form serve two functions for the reader: they elicit a set of expectations, and they provide a structure for the critical analysis of an individual selection. Traditional forms derived from primitive peoples in an oral mode include parables, fables, folk and fairy tales, myths, and legends. Modern forms are usually distinguished as realism or fantasy and are more complex than traditional forms.

Activities for Further Study

1. Ask students to identify as many literary forms as they know. Cite examples of each form.

---

[43]Elaine L. Konigsburg, *From the Mixed-Up Files of Mrs. Basil E. Frankweiler* (New York: Atheneum Publishers, 1967).

[44]Esther Forbes, *Johnny Tremain*, illustrated by Lynd Ward (Boston: Houghton Mifflin Co., 1943).

[45]Marguerite Henry, *King of the Wind*, illustrated by Wesley Dennis (Chicago: Rand McNally & Co., 1948).

[46]Keith Robertson, *Henry Reed's Babysitting Service*, illustrated by Robert McCloskey (New York: Viking Press, 1958).

[47]Lorenz Graham, *South Town* (Chicago: Follett Publishing Co., 1959).

[48]Zilpha Keatley Snyder, *The Egypt Game*, illustrated by Alton Raible (New York: Atheneum Publishers, 1967).

[49]Anne Holm, *North to Freedom*, (New York: Harcourt, Brace & World, 1965).

2. List several titles and several forms or genre. Ask students to match them. For example:

a) Little Match Girl   Fable
b) Jason and The Golden Fleece   Fairy tale
c) The Fox and The Grapes   Folktale
d) Three Billy Goats Gruff   Realistic fiction
e) Roosevelt Grady   Myth

3. List characteristics of several literary forms. Ask students to group them under the label of the form they describe. For example,

a) characters are usually animals
b) repetition of three incidents and three characters
c) deals with magical elements and the supernatural
d) characters and objects used to symbolize religious ideals
e) characters are farmers, soldiers, commonfolk
f) characters serve as symbols of a virtue or a folly
g) used to teach spiritual lesson
h) a representative slice of life

4. Compare several versions of the same folktale from different countries. List and discuss reasons that may account for similarities.
5. After reading several folktales, ask students to select the most interesting descriptive phrases; or to notice the use of rhyme or repetition.
6. Using Frye's four categories of novel, romance, anatomy, and confession, try to place several well-known children's books in them.

Selected References

ARBUTHNOT, MAY HILL. *Children and Books.* 3d ed. Chicago: Scott, Foresman & Co., 1964.

DANZIGER, MARLIES K., and JOHNSON, W. STACY. *An Introduction to Literary Criticism.* Lexington, Mass.: D. C. Heath & Co., 1961.

FRYE, NORTHROP. *Anatomy of Criticism.* Princeton, N. J.: Princeton University Press, 1957.

GEORGIOU, CONSTANTINE. *Children and Their Literature.* Englewood Cliffs, N. J.: Prentice-Hall, 1969.

HOLLOWELL, LILLIAN. *A Book of Children's Literature.* 3d ed. New York: Holt, Rinehart & Winston, 1966.

HUCK, CHARLOTTE, and KUHN, DORIS YOUNG. *Children's Literature in the Elementary School.* 2d ed. New York: Holt, Rinehart & Winston, 1968.

NESBITT, ELIZABETH. "The Critic and Children's Literature." *A Critical Approach to Children's Literature.* Edited by Sara Innis Fenwick. Chicago: University of Chicago Press, 1967.

OLSON, PAUL A., and HEDGES, NED S. "Analyzing Literature in the Elementary Institute." *Source Book on English Institutes for Elementary Teachers.* Champaign, Illinois: National Council of Teachers of English, 1965.

O'NEILL-BARNA, ANNE. "All in the Telling." *The New York Times Book Review*. November 9, 1969.

RESTON, JAMES. Editorial. *The New York Times*. February 14, 1969.

THOMPSON, STITH. *The Folktale*. New York: Holt, Rinehart & Winston, 1951.

WECHSLER, JAMES A. Editor. *New York Post*. February 14, 1969.

WELLEK, RENÉ, and WARREN, AUSTIN. *Theory of Literature*. 3d ed. New York: Harcourt, Brace & World, 1956.

Selected References for Children

FABLES

BROWN, MARCIA. *Once a Mouse . . . A Fable Cut in Wood*. New York: Charles Scribner's Sons, 1961.

COONEY, BARBARA, adapt. *Chanticleer and the Fox*. Illustrated by Barbara Cooney. New York: Thomas Y. Crowell Co., 1958.

LA FONTAINE, JEAN DE. *The Lion and the Rat*. Illustrated by Brian Wildsmith. New York: Franklin Watts, 1964.

———. *The Rich Man and the Shoemaker*. Illustrated by Brian Wildsmith. New York: Franklin Watts, 1965.

LIONNI, LEO. *Tico and the Golden Wings*. New York: Pantheon Books, 1964.

REEVES, JAMES, ed. *Fables of Aesop*. Illustrated by Maurice Wilson. New York: Henry Z. Walck, 1962.

THURBER, JAMES. *Fables for Our Time*. New York: Harper & Row, 1940.

UNTERMEYER, LOUIS, selector and adapter. *Aesop's Fables*. Illustrated by Alice and Martin Provensen. New York: Golden Books, 1965.

FANTASY

DAHL, ROALD. *Charlie and the Chocolate Factory*. Illustrated by Joseph Schindelman. New York: Alfred A. Knopf, 1964.

———. *James and the Giant Peach*. Illustrated by Nancy Ekholm Burkert. New York: Alfred A. Knopf, 1961.

GRAHAME, KENNETH. *The Wind in the Willows*. Illustrated by E. H. Shepard. New York: Charles Scribner's Sons, 1901, 1953.

KENDALL, CAROL. *The Gammage Cup*. Illustrated by Erik Blegvad. New York: Harcourt, Brace & World, 1959.

WHITE, E. B. *Charlotte's Web*. Illustrated by Garth Williams. New York: Harper & Row, 1952.

FOLK AND FAIRY TALES

ASBJÖRNSEN, PETER C., and MOE, J. E. *East of the Sun and West of the Moon*. Illustrated by Hedvig Collin. New York: Macmillan Co., 1928, 1963.

———. *Norwegian Folk Tales*. Translated by P. S. Iversen and Carl Norman. Illustrated by Erik Werenskiold and Theodor Kittelson. New York: Viking Press, 1845, 1961.

CAMPBELL, JOHN F. *Popular Tales of the West Highlands*. Detroit: Gale-Singing Tree Press, 1890-93.

CHASE, RICHARD. *The Jack Tales*. Illustrated by Berkeley Williams, Jr. Boston: Houghton Mifflin Co., 1943.

————. *The Grandfather Tales.* Illustrated by Berkeley Williams, Jr. Boston: Houghton Mifflin Co., 1948.

GRIMM, JACOB and WILHELM. *Grimm's Fairy Tales.* Translated by Margaret Hunt. Illustrated by children of 15 nations. Chicago: Follett Publishing Co., 1968.

HOLL, ADELAIDE. *The Rain Puddle.* Illustrated by Roger Duvoisin. New York: Lothrop, Lee & Shepard Co., 1965.

JACOBS, JOSEPH, collector. *English Fairy Tales.* Illustrated by John D. Batten. New York: Dover Publications, 1898, 1967.

MACMANUS, SEUMAS, comp. *Donegal Fairy Stories.* New York: Dover Publications, 1900.

————. *Hibernian Nights.* Illustrated by Paul Kennedy. New York: Macmillan Co., 1963.

O'SULLIVAN, SEAN, ed. and trans. *Folktales of Ireland.* Chicago: University of Chicago Press, 1966.

PICARD, BARBARA, comp. *German Hero Sagas and Folk Tales.* Illustrated by Joan Kiddell-Monroe. New York: Henry Z. Walck, 1958.

THOMPSON, STITH, comp. *One Hundred Favorite Folktales.* Bloomington, Indiana: Indiana University Press, 1968.

THURBER, JAMES. *Many Moons.* Illustrated by Louis Slobodkin. New York: Harcourt, Brace & World, 1944.

UCHIDA, YOSHIKO. *The Dancing Kettle and Other Japanese Folk Tales.* Illustrated by Richard C. Jones. New York: Harcourt, Brace & World, 1949.

UNTERMEYER, LOUIS and BRYNA. *Complete Grimm's Fairy Tales.* 2 vols. New York: Dial Press.

MYTHS AND LEGENDS

ASIMOV, ISAAC. *Words from the Myths.* Illustrated by William Barss. Boston: Houghton Mifflin Co., 1961.

COLUM, PADRAIC. *The Children of Odin.* Illustrated by Willy Pogany. New York: Macmillan Co., 1962.

————. *The Golden Fleece and the Heroes Who Lived before Achilles.* Illustrated by Willy Pogany. New York: Macmillan Co., 1942.

HOUSTON, JAMES. *The White Archer.* New York: Harcourt, Brace & World, 1967.

————. *Tikta'liktak: An Eskimo Legend.* New York: Harcourt, Brace & World, 1965.

PYLE, HOWARD. *Some Merry Adventures of Robin Hood, of Great Renown in Nottinghamshire.* New York: Charles Scribner's Sons, 1954.

TOOR, FRANCES. *The Golden Carnation; and Other Stories Told in Italy.* Illlustrated by Anne Marie Jauss. New York: Lothrop, Lee & Shepard Co., 1961.

TRESSELT, ALVIN, and CLEAVER, NANCY. *The Legend of the Willow Plate.* Illustrated by Joseph Low. New York: Parents' Magazine Press, 1968.

WARREN, ROBERT PENN. *The Gods of Mount Olympus.* Illustrated by William Moyers. New York: Random House, 1959.

NARRATIVE POETRY

LONGFELLOW, HENRY WADSWORTH. *Paul Revere's Ride.* Illustrated by Paul Galdone. New York: Thomas Y. Crowell Co., 1963.

REES, ENNIS. *The Song of Paul Bunyan and Tony Beaver*. Illustrated by Robert Osborn. New York: Pantheon Books, 1964.

PARABLES

LATOURETTE, JANE. *The House on the Rock*. Illustrated by Sally Matthews. St. Louis, Mo.: Concordia Publishing House, 1966.
————. *Jon and the Little Lost Lamb*. Illustrated by Betty Wind. St. Louis, Mo.: Concordia Publishing House, 1965.

REALISM

FORBES, ESTHER. *Johnny Tremain*. Illustrated by Lynd Ward. Boston: Houghton Mifflin Co., 1943.
GRAHAM, LORENZ. *South Town*. Chicago: Follett Publishing Co., 1959.
HENRY, MARGUERITE. *King of the Wind*. Illustrated by Wesley Dennis. Chicago: Rand McNally Co., 1948.
HOLM, ANNE. *North to Freedom*. New York: Harcourt, Brace & World, 1965.
KONIGSBURG, ELAINE L. *From the Mixed-Up Files of Mrs. Basil E. Frankweiler*. New York: Atheneum Publishers, 1967.
ROBERTSON, KEITH. *Henry Reed's Babysitting Service*. Illustrated by Robert McCloskey. New York: Viking Press, 1958.
SNYDER, ZILPHA KEATLEY. *The Egypt Game*. Illustrated by Alton Raible. New York: Atheneum Publishers, 1967.

chapter 3

components
of narrative fiction

Although there are various ways that one can approach the study of narrative fiction for children, the view adopted here is to consider the literary form, the components of theme, plot, setting and characterization, and writing style. Adults who select and interpret books with children will recognize the hallmarks of good writing as they evaluate the theme, characters, plot, and setting. A story must hold a child's attention or intrigue him enough to make him want to find out how it comes out, or else it will not be read. The criterion, "Does it tell a good story?", then, will be a necessary consideration for those selecting books for children. Characterization is equally important, for if the characters in the story appear believable and authentic in the world created by the author, both children and adults will be drawn to them.

Theme, which provides the underlying meaning in literature, is an elusive, yet integral and pervasive, component. It is highly indicative of quality in literature. Generally, children do not verbalize their recognition or appreciation of theme unless they have been guided in reading for deeper meanings. Setting is a more obvious component than theme, but it is used by the author in subtle ways to achieve his aesthetic purpose. Each element in a work of narrative fiction is a determinant of the others. As Henry James discussed the process through which his various novels took form, he frequently asked, in effect, What is character but the determination of incident, and what is incident but an illustration of character?[1] It is through the characters' actions as the plot develops that the theme is revealed, and for this reason, no single component can be considered in isolation from other components.

---

[1] Henry James, *The Art of the Novel: Critical Prefaces* (New York: Charles Scribner's Sons, 1934).

Realizing Literary Themes

From what has been said about the interdependency of literary elements, it should be apparent that a discussion of literary themes, apart from their interpenetration with plots, settings, and characters, is artificial. Each element, such as theme, must be viewed in its relation to the other elements. A plot tells the action, but a theme reveals the significance of the action; a theme tells the reader what an experience means. A theme is not merely the discourse or topic with which the author deals but is his message or comment on that topic as his story evolves. Hence, the significance and interpretation of the events and characters of the narration are pervaded by a sense of developing meaning. A piece of narrative fiction for children attains coherence as its theme, its characters, and its action yield a consistency with each other. Brooks and Warren speak of "the logic of theme" which they suggest is a "thematic structure into which the various elements are fitted and in terms of which they achieve unity."[2]

Seemingly, our psychological makeup demands a theme, a necessity for making sense of events, hence the structural equation: *no theme, no story.* The theme, then, transcends the characters and events of the story, but derives from the movement of all parts toward a significant end, some idea or feeling that is consistently developing throughout the story. Consequently, theme embodies a meaning or interpretation that is significant beyond the particular persons and events described.

In children's literature, theme is generally simpler than in adult literature; it embodies significance of experiences that children can understand. Furthermore, there is usually only one theme, whereas in adult literature, there may be several. Theme in children's literature has moral and ethical connotations, but it should not be concluded that it is a kind of moralizing with examples. Neither should it be thought that light and humorous stories that entertain are without themes. In good literature, as the characters act and as the plot unfolds, the meaning emerges from the experience. This meaning, which is the theme, can be stated explicitly, as in a fable, or implicitly, as in an allegory, a fantasy, or realistic fiction.

Appraising Themes. Editors of children's books, the persons who select stories for publication, as well as teachers and librarians who recommend these stories to children, base their judgments upon a number of criteria, including those which deal with themes. Among the

---

[2]Cleanth Brooks and Robert Penn Warren, *Understanding Fiction*, 2d ed. (New York: Appleton-Century-Crofts, 1959), p. 274. Copyright © 1959 by Educational Division, Meredith Corp. Reprinted with permission of Appleton-Century-Crofts.

principal criteria for themes are those that attend to external correspon-dence, or *relevance,* and those that are concerned with factors internal to the story, or *coherence.* Children's stories that are rejected because of *relevance* may be those whose themes are inappropriate to the world of reality or imagination of the child. Thus, stories dealing with intricate adult concerns, such as the dating problems of college girls, have little relevance for elementary school children. Clearly, the values or human conditions treated in such stories lack a basis for identification by the young child. Appraisals of relevance are, in general, easier to make than those based on coherence—the internal factors of theme. Internal unity is a requirement for excellence in both fiction and nonfiction, states one editor.

> Whether an author writes fiction or nonfiction, his sense of unity and coherence makes the whole a complete expression of the basic idea that grew out of his mind and experience. Unity, universality, and inevitability, we have all learned, are the common properties of every masterpiece. And a children's book must not partake any less of them than any other great work.[3]

Coherence of theme derives from the consistency of the story in its own right, the organization of plot, setting, characterization, and style to yield an expressive unity. Brooks and Warren suggest that

> . . . we may find that we have rejected the story not because of its theme as such, but because we have found the story unconvincing. The story failed in its logic of motivation, or in its presentation of character, or in the attempt to make the theme develop from the action. Or perhaps we have found the story guilty of sentimentality; that is, the emotional response demanded by the story is not really justified by the events in the story. In other words, we have rejected the story, not because of the theme, taken as a thing in itself, but because the story is incoherent as a story.[4]

The current demand for books about children of multi-ethnic back-grounds has resulted in a few excellent titles. The demand has also resulted in a rash of inadequate stories using acceptance as the central and emphatic theme, but with plot and theme lacking coherence. During the past twenty-five years, the number of books about Negro children has increased, but in some, the theme of acceptance overpowers other components of the writing. deAngeli's *Bright April,*[5] with a racial issue

---

[3]Jean Karl, "A Children's Editor Looks at Excellence in Children's Literature," *The Horn Book Magazine,* vol. 43 (February, 1967), pp. 34-35. Copyright © 1967 by The Horn Book, Inc. Reprinted with permission of The Horn Book, Inc.
[4]Brooks and Warren, *Understanding Fiction,* pp. 276-277.
[5]Marguerite deAngeli, *Bright April* (Garden City, N. Y.: Doubleday & Co., 1946).

in each episode and repeated use of the slogan, "Do your best," has been criticized on this account.

Themes which meet the criterion of coherence are usually marked by at least two properties. First, there is throughout the story the organic development of a feeling, attitude, or idea in which the experience conveyed provides a necessary and sufficient basis for the reader to accept the theme. Second, the theme is developed uniquely. For example, a subtle and powerful theme may never be stated explicitly but, rather, it pervades the writing in such a way that the sensitive reader is more impressed with it than if he were patently confronted with it. In John Donovan's book, *I'll Get There. It Better Be Worth the Trip*,[6] the theme is implicit in the title. Without being stated explicitly, the theme develops from the action. The reader is painfully aware that Davy, the hero, sees his route toward adulthood as a precarious trip, one that he must travel without much stable adult guidance. His childlike acceptance of the adults in his life conveys an insightful message for children who grow up in the midst of less-than-perfect adults.

Similarly, in *Shadow of a Bull*, Manolo Olivar faces life decisions that reveal a theme totally integrated into the plot, the characters, and the writing style. The conflict is described in the first paragraph, and Manolo's battle to become his own man permeates the entire story.

> When Manolo was nine he became aware of three important facts in his life. First: the older he became, the more he looked like his father. Second: he, Manolo Olivar, was a coward. Third: everyone in the town of Arcangel expected him to grow up to be a famous bullfighter, like his father.
> No one had to tell him these three things were true. He and everyone in the town of Arcangel knew the first and the last of these to be true. And the fact that he was a coward only he himself was aware of.[7]

Contrast the implicit themes with the statement rendered by an author of children's books who feared superficial readers. "I just couldn't live with the idea that a reader might not get my message. After all, it was the reason I wrote the story and so I had one of my characters say it outright." If the total integration exists, there is little need for an explicit statement of theme. If the total unity is missing, there is little hope for the story.

The second important property of theme is its unique development. Does this story give the reader a new perspective he had not known

---

6John Donovan, *I'll Get There. It Better Be Worth the Trip* (New York: Harper & Row, 1969).

7Maia Wojciechowska, *Shadow of a Bull* (New York: Atheneum Publishers, 1964) p. 3. Copyright © 1964 by Maia Wojciechowska. Used by permission of Atheneum Publishers.

Illustration by Alvin Smith, from Maia Wojciechowska's *Shadow of a Bull*. Copyright ©
1964 by Maia Wojciechowska. Used by permission of Atheneum Publishers.

before? Even though a theme may be a common idea, its development in a story permits it to emerge as something unique and memorable. The ingenuity with which the theme is illustrated in a story makes it noteworthy. By casting the activities of a child finding something to do into a larger frame of reference of finding a place for oneself, Ann Herbert Scott brings a fresh look at familiar relationships in *Sam*.[8] Sam is repeatedly rejected by each member of his family in situations that most children know. Despite the familiar situations and the familiar need-to-be-accepted theme, Ann Herbert Scott's portrayal of it is fresh and imaginative.

Certainly, the significance of literature is measured in part by the uniqueness with which the theme is presented. Scott O'Dell's Newbery Award winner, *Island of the Blue Dolphins*,[9] portrays a theme of survival through forgiveness of one's enemies. In this story, Karana is required, in order to survive, to accept forces that had deprived her of her family. By revealing not only her stoic actions, but her thoughts and feelings, the author changes a historical chronicle into a narrative with a powerful theme. Karana's quiet courage comes through the first person narration to raise this story above the ordinary.

Burton says:

> The basic difference between the journalistic novel and that which rises above it lies probably in the complexity of characters and in the presence of an idea (or ideas) which gives unity to events. What a soldier did in a war is less important than why he did it, and in the great novel he becomes a symbol of humanity.[10]

John Steptoe conveys a nostalgic theme from an unusual vantage point in *Stevie*,[11] excerpted in the next chapter. His theme is concern for another person even though he may be a bother and a pest at times. Robert found fault with nearly everything Stevie did, but his continuous criticism is stilled when Stevie's parents move and take him away. No theme is explicitly stated in this book but, when Robert's bowl of corn flakes gets soggy, the reader shares his loneliness as the boy realizes that Stevie won't return again. Steptoe has done more than to *say* Robert misses Stevie, he has *shown* it. A theme demonstrated through plot and characters carries a greater impact than one stated explicitly.

---

[8]Ann Herbert Scott, *Sam*, illustrated by Symeon Shimin (New York: McGraw-Hill Book Co., 1967).

[9]Scott O'Dell, *Island of the Blue Dolphins* (Boston: Houghton Mifflin Co., 1960).

[10]Dwight L. Burton, *Literature Study in the High Schools* (New York: Holt, Rinehart & Winston, 1963), p. 103.

[11]John Steptoe, *Stevie* (New York: Harper & Row, 1969).

Illustration by Symeon Shimin, from Ann Herbert Scott's *Sam*. Copyright © 1967 by Ann Herbert Scott and Symeon Shimin. Used by permission of McGraw-Hill Book Co.

Defining Plot

The interdependency of the components of literature needs to be recalled before beginning a discussion of plot. For characterization, theme, and setting are manifested through the plot which is developed through the author's style. The plot in fiction is the scheme of narration; it is the development of the sequence of episodes. To the child reader, all other elements tend to be subordinate to the narration of events. A book that does not tell a good story has little appeal for children. Without an engaging plot, even the most sensitive descriptions are lost as a child's attention wanes from the narration of action. Isaac Singer underscores the child's demand for an engaging story:

> It's a lot easier to hypnotize grown-ups than children. It's easier to force university students to eat literary straw and clay than an infant in a kindergarten. No child can be influenced by tortured criticism or quotes from authorities. No child is altruistic enough to read a book because it might help society or progress. The child is still selfish to demand an interesting story. He wants surprises and tensions.[12]

The surprises and tensions created by an author flow from an intelligible plot to sustain the interest of the young reader. A well-constructed plot contains a set of discernible actions arranged in a logical pattern leading to a climax and denouement. The episodes within a plot are structured toward an aesthetic purpose which brings about an overall coherence and effect. Generally, the action is stronger in children's literature than in adult literature, or there is more use of scene, with a summary used to add any information the reader needs for understanding the scene. Furthermore, in children's literature, characterization is less developed and less complex than in adult literature, and so the action must be stronger to maintain interest.

Librarians attest to the fact that some Newbery Award books are readily dismissed by children and that they rarely circulate from library shelves. The stories may not appeal because there is not enough action and suspense to hold attention. A children's editor offered the following suggestions about the requirements for plot in children's literature:

> The author of a book of fiction, especially fiction for children, needs a sense of plot. He needs to know, by the time he has finished writing at least, how and where his story begins, what the climax is, and how it ends. He needs to know that a plot is not a series of progressive incidents of equal value leading from here to there with

---

[12]Isaac Bashevis Singer, "I See the Child as a Last Refuge," in *The New York Times Book Review* (November 9, 1969), p. 66. Copyright © by the New York Times Company. Reprinted by permission.

no complications. In a children's book, plot is a problem that grows, generally, out of character and is resolved by the efforts of the hero or heroine. It has suspense, action, and life.[13]

A good storyteller captures the interest of his audience, tells the significant incidents in an understandable order, and delivers the climax and ending after the appropriate suspense is built up. These requirements of stories for children do not differ notably, whether the story is told orally or in print, for the same features of unity, coherence, and completeness distinguish both oral and graphic presentations. Unnecessary and irrelevant details clog a story line and interfere with understanding.

The plot, then, is the structure of a scheme of events presented in the story. It necessarily involves the characters' actions in sequential episodes that permit the theme of the story to emerge. While such a general stipulation is true of all literature, both child and adult, some distinguishing features mark literature for children. In the following sections, these features will be noted and examples offered.

The Structure of Plots. Plot structure is the design of the sequence of events in a story; it is the development of the story's surprises and tensions which should provide a continuous process of significant discovery. Stories are arranged through numerous designs, with the choice of sequence a significant element of the storytelling. When a story is told from the point of view of one of the characters, he and the reader discover facts and features within the plot at the same time. Sequence, of course, does not here mean the real chronology of events but, rather, the use the author makes of events to develop the action and unity of the story. This selection of events does manifest some purposeful order, but the order derives from the author's aesthetic purpose and his decision as to how the story is best told. Consequently, the plot narrative may be noticeably artificial when contrasted with the natural chronology of events. Thus, stories may begin in the middle or near the end of an actual sequence of happenings in time.

The narrative structure is built with smaller units, such as episodes and incidents, and is generally not as complex in children's literature as it is in adult literature. No matter where the story starts in describing the action, the reader's interest must be captured early so that he becomes involved and cares about what happens to the characters of the story.

Order of Narration. In most simple terms, every story may be said to have a beginning, a middle, and an ending. The more extensive terms

---

[13]Karl, "A Children's Editor," p. 33.

of summary, narrative, analysis, and scene appropriate to a study of adult literature would be largely superfluous for children's literature, but some useful parallels may be drawn between the basic ways order is arranged in literary plots. The *beginning* of a story involves exposition which introduces the reader to an unsettled state of affairs. A preparation is made for involving the reader in an anomaly, a problem, conflict, or lack of symmetry in the events of narration. This may emerge from the description of the characters, or the setting, or something of the dialogue itself. The author's style determines how it is achieved. Highlighting this point for children who would be writers, Elizabeth Yates notes:

> A story demands an immediate beginning. In the first lines, first two or three paragraphs, half-page, the reader's attention is to be won; descriptions of the time and place of the story, or the conflict that is to be resolved, may all be necessary, but they will be rightly met further on. The reader wants to know where he is; what he wants to do is to get into stride as quickly as possible with the characters who make up the story, and start living their lives.[14]

The *middle,* or complication of the story, develops the conflict or disequilibrium mentioned above. It usually involves action toward equilibrium. The *ending,* or resolution, includes denouement or climax and indicates the disposition of the conflict situation. After the climax, there is usually a tapering off or a settling down to a normal state. The conclusion, "they lived happily ever after," is usually reserved for classic fairy tales in children's literature, but frequently, the identical thought is evident in other types of fiction. The relationship of the phases of a story may be either vividly apparent or without strong lines of demarcation. What is important, of course, is the unity and coherence of their presentation. Again, Yates contends that:

> The end of a story grows out of the beginning and is in direct relation to it. It has been happening all through the story as the seeds sown early grew and matured and were gathered into the harvest. Some may have been gathered sooner than others, but all were counted in. Characters played out their parts; events served their various purposes; conflicts were resolved; the main character solved the most difficult problem and merited a reward. It has been logical within the wide bounds of imagination, not coincidental. There is nothing left to be said by the writer, for a careful ending leaves no unanswered questions; but there is a great deal for the reader to go on thinking about.[15]

---

[14]Elizabeth Yates, *Someday You'll Write* (New York: E. P. Dutton & Co., 1962), p. 33. Copyright © 1962 by Elizabeth Yates McGreal. Reprinted by permission of E. P. Dutton & Co., Inc.

[15]Ibid., p. 36.

The beginning, then, is used to pique interest, to make the reader care about what happens, and the ending must contain a satisfactory resolution of the obstacles, problems, or conflicts presented. What happens between the presentation of the issue and the resolution of the problems is a series of episodes containing conflicts, discoveries, reversals, and intrigue. If each episode advances the action, the child reader will continue to read the story. Sperry demonstrates a clean plot line in *Call It Courage*.[16] He starts the tale as if it were a legend told long ago by the Polynesians and ends with the same paragraph, except for one line. Noteworthy is how the chapter headings reveal the significant phases of the plot line development. The headings are: "Flight," "The Sea," "The Island," "Drums," and "Homeward." Only events necessary for the reader's understanding are told of a boy's struggle to become courageous and of his efforts to prove it to his father. By his arrangement of the material, the author adds measurably to the feeling that the story is an authentic legend.

The order of the narration may begin at any point in the sequence of events. An author reorders episodes to achieve the desired suspense, to give background information, or to heighten interest. A restructuring of the chronological order and returning to prior events to bring the reader up-to-date is called a flashback. Flash-backs are not used frequently, since children may have difficulty keeping a story in order in their minds, although Emily Neville used it successfully in two books —*Berries Goodman* and *The Seventeenth-Street Gang*.[17]

The design of plot structure may be cumulative, episodic, cyclic, rising and falling action, or gradual development. The cumulative tale goes to the beginning and rebuilds the story with the addition of each new event. *Drummer Hoff*[18] is a recent example which demonstrates the use of accumulation of events to build up to the resounding climax. In another frequently used plot structure, the episodic form, each chapter is centered on a small conflict or event. Though *Homer Price*[19] illustrates an interesting collection of episodes woven together through the use of a central character, the episodic form is often poorly used because it does not build toward a satisfactory climax. Whatever structural plan is used, the ending must satisfy what has gone before it. Some folktales illustrate the cyclic nature of plot structures. The plot generally

---

[16]Armstrong Sperry, *Call It Courage* (New York: Macmillan Co., 1940).
[17]Emily Neville, *Berries Goodman* (New York: Harper & Row, 1965). *The Seventeenth-Street Gang* (New York: Harper & Row, 1966).
[18]Barbara Emberley, *Drummer Hoff,* illustrated by Ed Emberley (Englewood Cliffs, N. J.: Prentice-Hall, 1967).
[19]Robert McCloskey, *Homer Price* (New York: Viking Press, 1943).

Illustration by Ed Emberley from *Drummer Hoff* by Barbara Emberley. Copyright © 1967 by Edward R. Emberley and Barbara Emberley. Used by permission of Prentice-Hall, Inc.

has three characters and three events which repeat one after the other. The rhythm and repetition of events lead to a satisfactory conclusion.

Credibility of Incidents. The credibility of plot is determined by the logical nature of events and the consistency of the narrative. That a plot is consistent within itself—like theme—requires that the experience it creates for a child's imagination be coherent. And so the logical plot involves change and development, tensions and complications that are plausible but not predictable. Children seek intrigue and fascination in their literature but not fortuitous coincidence. Thus, the heroine who is regularly saved from harrowing encounters by her detective father becomes palpably preposterous. The presence of a *deus ex machina* is no more acceptable in children's fiction than it is in adult literature, unless the form permits it, such as in Greek tragedy.

Even in fantasy, or perhaps especially in fantasy, the improbable must occur within the framework of possibility that the author has established. Huck and Kuhn describe many techniques authors use to create fantasy worlds, and they cite methods that help create belief in those worlds.[20] The author's fidelity to the details of the fantasy world is necessary to convey the feeling of credibility. Isaac Singer insists on logical plots and consistency in children's literature.

> Stories for children are now being written without a beginning, middle or end. Their writers seem to believe that children have no head for logic. They see the child's mind as basically Kafkaesque. Actually youngsters are extremely logical. They may accept premises which don't agree with the adult image of reality, but once they have accepted a premise, the action that follows must be strictly logical. Children ask questions which adults no longer dare to ask. They demand consistency, clarity, precision and other obsolete qualities.[21]

To summarize, children's books require credibility of plot.

Corollary to the requirement that a plot be credible is the expectation that it must be based on some element of novelty, surprise, or the unexpected. Just as children are not susceptible to undue coincidence, neither are they interested in plots that are pedestrian and predictable. They have little desire to read about others whose lives seem to plod along in routine ways. The ingenuity that an author uses to unravel the intricacies of the plot must hold the reader's interest, or the book is tossed aside. A mood of suspense can be created and sustained by the manner in which an author initiates the plot. Alta Hal-

---

[20]Charlotte Huck and Doris Young Kuhn, *Children's Literature in the Elementary School,* 2d ed. (New York: Holt, Rinehart & Winston, 1968), pp. 338-370.
[21]Singer, "I See the Child," p. 66.

verson Seymour quickly engages the interest of her readers in *Toward Morning*. A preteen for whom reading fiction was not active enough was captured by the excitement and intrigue in this story of Teresa and Janos, members of the Hungarian Freedom Fighters.

> "What are you going to do, Janos?" Teresa Nagy's eyes were anxious as she watched her tall brother pull on his coat and stand waiting at the sitting-room window of their little apartment that October day in Budapest. Janos had a tense, determined look that made Teresa sure something definite and probably dangerous was in the making. She had suspected it for several days—days when he had stayed longer than usual at the college, had brought home a group of young students to spend hours in his small room, talking, talking, talking in earnest voices. "Hungary has got to strike for freedom, and there's no use waiting!" she had heard them say.[22]

The reader is immediately caught up in the problem and action of this plot.

The increasing amount of realism in children's literature is undoubtedly an improvement over the sugar and spice books of the past, but realism in and of itself is not enough to appeal to any reader. Presenting real social problems merely for the sake of realism results in situations that are commonplace and that hold little interest. Literature for children needs to have a judicious blending of what is novel and unusual with what is known and familiar. The skill of an author is either highlighted or defaulted by the manner in which he sketches his plot line to meet these requirements. Uniqueness is revealed in an excellent piece of literature and this, among other features, distinguishes it from the ordinary.

Identifying Believable Characterization

Characterization, a significant component of children's literature, is one the adult critic will evaluate. It includes a description of the traits and behavior of the central figures in a story, figures which may be toads, steam shovels, a variety of make-believe figures, or human beings. J. N. Hook identified nine techniques that an author might use in describing a character to the reader. They are (1) telling about the character, (2) describing the character and his surroundings, (3) showing the character in action, (4) letting the character talk, (5) revealing the character's thoughts, (6) showing what others say to the char-

---

[22]Alta Halverson Seymour, *Toward Morning* (Chicago: Follett Publishing Co., 1961), p. 7. Copyright © 1961 by Alta Halverson Seymour. Reprinted with permission of Follett Publishing Co.

acter, (7) showing what others say about the character, (8) showing the reactions of others to the character, and (9) showing the character's reactions to others.[23]

Authors of literature for primary grade children use action and dialogue as the main techniques to establish characters. In literature for older children, authors use each of these techniques in various combinations to capture the essence of a character in words. Many factors combine to determine the extent to which a character is developed. Characterization, of course, is influenced by choice of genre. Fairy tales require characters that are all good or all bad; fables generally require animal characters that symbolize a human weakness or virtue. There is little change in character, since they represent something else. Some of the most memorable characters have come from fantasies and realistic stories in which the character is so thoroughly developed that he exerts a form of control over the events of the story. It is said that once the characters are described and the form and style chosen, the story is known. Wellek and Warren describe three approaches to characterization.

> Modes of characterization are many. Older novelists like Scott introduce each of their major persons by a paragraph describing in detail the physical appearance and another analyzing the moral and psychological nature. But this form of block characterization may be reduced to an introductory label. Or the label may turn into a device of mimicry or pantomime—some mannerism, gesture, or saying, which, as in Dickens, recurs whenever the character reappears, serving as emblematic accompaniment. Mrs. Gummidge is "always thinking of the old un"; Uriah Heep has a word, "umble," and also a ritual gesture of the hands. Hawthorne sometimes characterizes by a literal emblem: Zenobia's red flower; Westervelt's brilliantly artificial teeth. The later James of *The Golden Bowl* has one character see another in symbolic terms.[24]

When an author has developed a fictional character thoroughly, the latter is endowed with such constraints and potential for action that he purportedly seems quite real to his creator. Pamela Travers remarked that she cried all over her typewriter the last time Mary Poppins went away. Elizabeth Yates has said that characters she created told their story to her and she merely recorded what they told her. She contends that once she has created the structure of the story and given the characters the breath of life, they create the action and the dialogue.

---

[23]J. N. Hook, *Writing Creatively* (Boston: D. C. Heath & Co., 1963), pp. 141-152.
    [24]René Wellek and Austin Warren, *Theory of Literature*, 3d ed. (New York: Harcourt, Brace & World, 1956), p. 219. Copyright © 1956 by Harcourt, Brace & World, Inc. and reprinted with their permission.

In examining characterization, several points need emphasis. These are the elements of credibility, character portrayal, and the individuality-universality of the characters presented.

Credibility of Characters. Characters described in a literary work need only to be believable within the framework of that story. They need to cause the action in the story to happen instead of merely being the objects that get acted upon. Characterization revealed through action in adult and children's literature differs on some counts. Olson and Hedges contrast characterization from their point of view.

> Characters in children's literature seldom have any pasts or inner selves, any complex system of motivation. They generally do not have any basis for acting which is not transparent. Their actions result from a dominant moral or social characteristic (ruling passion); or they are the fruit of present decision. Rarely are characters in children's books motivated by necessity, habit, or an impulse imposed by the past. Of course, the people whom children see, they see as pretty much without a past. These characters, were they found in novels, would be called "flat characters" in Forster's sense, a sense which need not carry pejorative connotations. The characters tend toward the condition of allegory. They become "figurae" for something else. Usually, one should ask what they stand for, not what (beyond the obvious) makes them tick. To remark over and over concerning such characters that they are very realistic and "human" and true to life (almost any character can be so seen) is not very helpful.[25]

In a child's novel, only a few characters are well-developed, since children are unable to keep a number of complex characters in mind. Moreover, action is more interesting to children than character studies. And so, roundly-developed characters are played off from flat characters, with little attention to incidental characters who move through a story. For example, characterization in *The Jazz Man*[26] reveals little about the past of any of the people. The reader is brought into the story at the present, although Zeke remembers that he has not always lived in Harlem, and little is explained about Zeke's not attending school. The reader is given glimpses of the kinds of jobs Zeke's Daddy likes but cannot keep. He is told that Zeke's Mama rocks him and reads to him, but that she leaves without telling him she is going. The reader knows nothing about the Jazz Man who would spread his big fingers across the piano keys and make the big box sing. It would "cry like a lone-

---

[25]Paul A. Olson and Ned S. Hedges, "Analyzing Literature in the Elementary Institute," in *Source Book on English Institutes for Elementary Teachers* (Champaign, Ill.: National Council of Teachers of English, 1965), p. 37.
[26]Mary Hays Weik, *The Jazz Man*, illustrated by Ann Grifalconi (New York: Atheneum Publishers, 1966), p. 14.

some child at night" and could explain things to Zeke "that nobody in the world had ever talked to him about before, that explained everything that had ever happened in his whole life." In this story, it is not necessary to know details about the Jazz Man's background; his music is more important than he is for the development of the action.

More of the inner life of the character is revealed in *Plain Girl*,[27] the story of an Amish family. The story focuses on Esther and is primarily one of inner conflict, revealed through her thoughts and conversation more than through her actions. Esther's father, her brother Dan, and her Aunt Ruth serve important functions in the story, and yet they do not detract from the central character, Esther. The author focuses on Esther's gradual changes as the plot unfolds; her personal development *is* the story. Esther recognizes that she and her brother can accept changes in their life without detracting from the tenets of the Amish religion.

Further requirements for character delineation and development are made according to the genre or type of literature. In realistic fiction, characters remain realistic and obey the laws of nature. The author of fantasy, who has greater freedom when creating his world, must make his characters remain within the chosen framework. *The Borrowers*,[28] tiny people who inhabit the space between walls, accomplish those feats appropriate to their size. Stuart Little does only what a tiny mouse boy could do.[29]

Portrayal of Character. Character delineation and character development are two related but separable aspects of characterization. Clear delineation sets the character apart with unique habits and characteristics so that the reader recognizes him or his actions immediately. In Forster's terms, both flat and round characters may be delineated clearly, but only round characters are developed.[30] Character development is the way an author shows that a character is not the same at the end of the story as he was at the beginning. Furthermore, it is his way of revealing more than one dimension of a character. By contrasting *Madeline*[31] and *Peter Rabbit*,[32] the differences in the extent of character development can be illustrated. Both characters are clearly delineated. Madeline is a daredevil who cares little for the feelings of others; Peter Rabbit will test the limits of any restrictions. Madeline is still the

---

[27]Virginia Sorenson, *Plain Girl* (New York: Harcourt, Brace & World, 1955).
[28]Mary Norton, *The Borrowers* (New York: Harcourt, Brace & World, 1953).
[29]E. B. White, *Stuart Little* (New York: Harper & Row, 1945).
[30]E. M. Forster, *Aspects of the Novel* (New York: Harcourt, Brace & World, 1927, 1955).
[31]Ludwig Bemelmans, *Madeline* (New York: Viking Press, 1939).
[32]Beatrix Potter, *The Tale of Peter Rabbit* (New York: Frederick Warne & Co., 1901).

same outspoken and tart youngster at the end of her story; but Peter appears to be slightly subdued as a result of his escapade. Both characters were clearly delineated, but only Peter Rabbit showed character development.

Character delineation and development are a function of the author's style and intent. By exposing many dimensions of some characters and by caricaturing others, an author makes them fit into the world he creates and makes them act toward his ultimate goal in the narrative. Neither good nor bad connotations should be associated with flat or round characters, for both are necessary. An author who is caught up in developing every character fully may achieve only a character study but never get a story told. Characters without action are not likely to appeal to children. Both flat and round characters are memorable and are subject to the author's purpose in the total structure. As Forster states:

> One great advantage of flat characters is that they are easily recognized whenever they come in—recognized by the reader's emotional eye, not by the visual eye, which merely notes the recurrence of a proper name. In Russian novels, where they so seldom occur, they would be a decided help. It is a convenience for an author when he can strike with his full force at once, and flat characters are very useful to him, since they never need reintroducing, never run away, have not to be watched for development, and provide their own atmosphere. . . .[33]

Books for children usually have at least one character who is fully described, and most often, the reader identifies with him. Character development and a realistic presentation of life are increasingly appearing in children's books. This trend contrasts sharply with children's novels written in the early 1900's when rounded characters were rarely depicted; good children were saccharine sweet, and the bad ones were monstrously bad.

Uniqueness of Character. Characterization is one of the principal avenues through which children become involved with their literature. By identifying with a character, a child can immerse himself totally in a story. In effect, he becomes the character with whom he is identifying. In order that children can empathize with characters and become engaged in literature, the characters must possess identifiable qualities to which children can relate, and yet perform authentically in the framework the author has built. The character must be an individual as each human being is an individual, unique and distinct from all other human beings. Still, the character must possess some universal qualities common

---

[33]Forster, "Aspects of the Novel."

to *all mankind* without becoming a stereotype. The steadfastness of a friend and the naïve acceptance of that friendship characterize Charlotte and Wilbur in *Charlotte's Web*.[34] When children have known these qualities in people in their own lives, they can accept the book characters as believable. Children recognize some of Charlotte's characteristics in their friends, or is it the other way around? Perhaps they see their human friends personified in Charlotte. The skillful author makes his characters unique and yet representative of basic human qualities. The character types personified by Mole, Water Rat, Badger, and Toad[35] can be found in most gatherings of human beings. Similarly, while Samantha in *Sam, Bangs and Moonshine*[36] is a unique and unusual child, she possesses qualities and exhibits behavioral traits that allow many children to identify with her. Her tendency to use make-believe moonshine talk, unmindful of the trouble it may cause, demonstrates behavior characteristically associated with childhood.

Recognizing Setting

Narrative fiction requires a choice of setting, a time and place for the sequence of action to occur. The principle of unity demands that the setting be interrelated with the characters and the theme. Some works aim at establishing and maintaining a mood through setting—a pervasive tone which is promoted by the description of the surroundings. Just as an author selects certain events and orders them in some way to develop his plot, so, too, he provides a place and a time in which the events occur. Often, the exposition of a story deals largely with setting, but setting pervades, in various degrees, all phases of a story. Setting may develop or change through the actions of a character in a story. For example, in *Where the Wild Things Are*,[37] Max creates and changes the setting with his vivid imagination when he is sent to bed without his supper.

The author, then, decides what is significant about the setting and what contributes to his purpose and to the credibility of the action. He may want to create the feeling of universality, such as the village in *Dorp Dead*,[38] which could be any village, or he may want to describe

---

[34]E. B. White, *Charlotte's Web,* illustrated by Garth Williams (New York: Harper & Row, 1952).

[35]Kenneth Grahame, *The Wind in the Willows,* illustrated by E. H. Shepard (New York: Charles Scribner's Sons, 1908).

[36]Evaline Ness, *Sam, Bangs and Moonshine* (New York: Holt, Rinehart & Winston, 1966).

[37]Maurice Sendak, *Where the Wild Things Are* (New York: Harper & Row, 1963).

[38]Julia Cunningham, *Dorp Dead,* illustrated by James Spanfeller (New York: Pantheon Books, a division of Random House, Inc., 1965).

Illustration by James Spanfeller, from Julia Cunningham's *Dorp Dead*. Copyright © 1965 by Julia Cunningham. Used by permission of Pantheon Books, a division of Random House, Inc.

a very specific place. He may use setting as environment, as Cunningham does with Mr. Kobalt's house in *Dorp Dead*. Wellek and Warren discuss this use of setting.

> Setting is environment; and environments, especially domestic interiors, may be viewed as metonymic, or metaphoric, expressions of character. A man's house is an extension of himself. Describe it and you have described him.[39]

Cunningham uses the orderliness of Kobalt's house, the routine and methodical work of ladder-making, and the ringing of the bells controlled by clocks to illustrate the nature of the man.

---

[39]Wellek and Warren, "Theory of Literature," p. 43.

In children's literature, the credibility of setting is not judged by physical accuracy, but by the mental or psychological fidelity of the setting created. In art, *seeming* real is more important than *being* real. Particularly in fantasies, the authenticity depends upon the author's skill in detailing the description of the setting. Setting may be used symbolically as in *Huckleberry Finn*[40] and in *The Cabin Faced West*.[41] It may become a character or an acting role in the scheme of events. Because both families live near the Mason-Dixon line in *The Perilous Road*[42] by Steele and *Across Five Aprils*[43] by Hunt, the central characters have brothers fighting for the North and for the South in the Civil War.

Literature for older children generally has more intricate and fully described settings than books for primary grade children. Consequently, setting occupies a proportionately larger part of the story in juvenile literature for older children. In *Constance*,[44] for example, Patricia Clapp details the setting of early Plymouth through the diary of the title character. Setting can also influence the regional appeal of a book for children. The setting in *The Pushcart War*[45] is easily identifiable for children in New York City, who see pushcarts frequently, but not for children elsewhere. Setting is often revealed through regional dialect or colloquial expressions. Louisa Shotwell provides clues to setting through language such as "the room got as still as piney woods" and "there was one thing about putting into that he purely had to find out."[46]

Setting is sometimes used as the central feature in a story, as it is in *Evan's Corner*.[47] Evan lived with three sisters, two brothers and his mother and father in two rooms, and so there was no place for him to be alone or to call his own. Evan found "a place of his own" but discovered that the place alone was not all that he needed for happiness.

Setting also plays an important role in *High-Rise Secret*[48] wherein the author makes the reader conscious of the realities of a housing

---

[40]Mark Twain, *Adventures of Huckleberry Finn* (New York: Harper & Row, 1884, 1931).

[41]Jean Fritz, *The Cabin Faced West*, illustrated by Feodor Rojankovsky (New York: Coward-McCann, 1958).

[42]William O. Steele, *The Perilous Road*, illustrated by Paul Galdone (New York: Harcourt, Brace & World, 1958).

[43]Irene Hunt, *Across Five Aprils*, illustrated by Albert John Pucci (Chicago: Follett Publishing Co., 1964).

[44]Patricia Clapp, *Constance: A Story of Early Plymouth* (New York: Lothrop Lee & Shepard Co., 1968).

[45]Jean Merrill, *The Pushcart War*, illustrated by Ronni Solbert (New York: William R. Scott, 1964).

[46]Louisa Shotwell, *Roosevelt Grady*, illustrated by Peter Burchard (New York: World Publishing Co., 1963).

[47]Elizabeth Starr Hill, *Evan's Corner*, illustrated by Nancy Grossman (New York: Holt, Rinehart & Winston, 1967).

[48]Lois Lenski, *High-Rise Secret* (Philadelphia: J. B. Lippincott Co., 1966).

Illustration by Nancy Grossman, from Elizabeth Starr Hill's *Evan's Corner*. Copyright © 1967 by Nancy Grossman. Used by permission of Holt, Rinehart & Winston, Inc.

project environment. In the beginning, the Murphys are unhappy in the immense, foreboding, impersonal highrise apartment building. The children are homesick for their familiar neighborhood, and Mrs. Murphy does not feel at home with the project's modern conveniences. The children are more open to change, and they delight in exploring the unfamiliar surroundings. The first person they meet is Frank, who is doing the housework because his father left home and his mother works. In their new environment, the Murphys cannot remain sheltered as they meet vandalism, racism, welfare, and alcoholism. The realities of the environment influence the development of their values and attitudes; Peggy fights Vernon when he insults Frank's dignity about eating surplus food; she ignores Peter when he snatches food from stores, attributing it to his homesickness. In this story, as in many by Lois Lenski, the environment plays a significant role.

Summary

Plot, theme, characterization, and setting are the primary elements of narrative fiction. The author's purpose for narrating a story (theme), the structures within which he works (plot) as he conveys his interpretation of a theme through setting, and the actions of individuals (characterization) are examined both separately and in relation to each other. The interdependence of the elements is emphasized, and the quality of their integration is suggested as a basis for appraising books for children. Although these literary elements also mark adult literature, their use and emphasis in writing for children constitute an appropriately different set of criteria for judging merit.

Theme portrays the author's purpose for writing the story and reveals the significance of the action he relates. Themes are judged for their external relevance and internal coherence. Plot requirements include action, interest, and suspense. The order in which an author tells his story, the point of view from which it is told, and the credibility of the incidents provide bench marks for evaluation. Requirements for characterization differ according to genre and the level of symbolization used. An author's style determines the mode used to present characterization; his aesthetic purpose determines the extent to which characters are developed; and his knowledge of mankind determines the sensitiveness with which he portrays human qualities. Setting is viewed as an extension of character, as a symbolic device, and as a means of establishing credibility.

Activities for Further Study

CHARACTERIZATION

1. Read, from several different books, paragraphs describing the main characters. Ask students which ones appeal to them. Analyze with them why the character appeals to them.
2. Read selections in which authors use different techniques for describing characterization. See if students can identify the techniques and use them to describe characters they know.

SETTING

1. Contrast the ways the setting is evoked in a realistic story and in a fantasy, such as Sheila Moon's *Knee Deep in Thunder* and Alan Garner's *Elidor.*
2. Have students select phrases that reveal setting. Discuss those phrases which present vivid mental images.

PLOT

1. List the sequence of events in a highly predictable series book. Compare this to the plot structure of Konigsburg's *The Mixed-Up Files of Mrs. Basil E. Frankweiler.*
2. Compare the sequence of events in O'Dell's *Island of the Blue Dolphins* and Sperry's *Call It Courage.*

THEME

1. Read several books with similar themes and compare the treatments. Read Donovan's *I'll Get There. It Better Be Worth the Trip*, Wojciechowska's *Shadow of a Bull*, and Hunt's *Across Five Aprils.* Contrast the life decisions each boy had to make.

Selected References

BROOKS, CLEANTH, and WARREN, ROBERT PENN. *Understanding Fiction.* 2d ed. New York: Appleton-Century-Crofts, Educational Division, Meredith Corp., 1959.

BURTON, DWIGHT L. *Literature Study in the High Schools.* New York: Holt, Rinehart & Winston, 1963.

FORSTER, E. M. *Aspects of the Novel.* New York: Harcourt, Brace & World, 1927, 1955.

HOOK, J. N. *Writing Creatively.* Boston: D. C. Heath & Co., 1963.

HUCK, CHARLOTTE, and KUHN, DORIS YOUNG. *Children's Literature in the Elementary School.* 2d ed. New York: Holt, Rinehart & Winston, 1968.

JAMES, HENRY. *The Art of the Novel: Critical Prefaces.* New York: Charles Scribner's Sons, 1934.

KARL, JEAN. "A Children's Editor Looks at Excellence in Children's Litera-
ture." *The Horn Book Magazine*, vol. 43, February 1967, pp. 33-35.
OLSON, PAUL A., and HEDGES, NED S. "Analyzing Literature in the Elementary
Institute." *Source Book on English Institutes for Elementary Teachers.*
Champaign, Ill.: National Council of Teachers of English, 1965.
SINGER, ISAAC BASHEVIS. "I See the Child as a last Refuge." *The New York
Times Book Review*, November 9, 1969.
WELLEK, RENÉ, and WARREN, AUSTIN. *Theory of Literature.* 3d ed. New
York: Harcourt, Brace & World, 1956.

Selected References for Children

BEMELMANS, LUDWIG. *Madeline.* New York: Viking Press, 1939.
CLAPP, PATRICIA. *Constance: A Story of Early Plymouth.* New York: Lothrop,
Lee & Shepard, 1968.
CUNNINGHAM, JULIA. *Dorp Dead.* Illustrated by James Spanfeller. New York:
Pantheon Books, 1965.
DEANGELI, MARGUERITE. *Bright April.* Garden City, N. Y.: Doubleday & Co.,
1946.
DONOVAN, JOHN. *I'll Get There. It Better Be Worth the Trip.* New York:
Harper & Row, 1969.
EMBERLEY, BARBARA. *Drummer Hoff.* Illustrated by Ed Emberley. Englewood
Cliffs, N. J.: Prentice-Hall, 1967.
FRITZ, JEAN. *The Cabin Faced West.* Illustrated by Feodor Rojankovsky. New
York: Coward-McCann, 1958.
GRAHAME, KENNETH. *The Wind in the Willows.* Illustrated by E. H. Shepard.
New York: Charles Scribner's Sons, 1908.
HILL, ELIZABETH STARR. *Evan's Corner.* Illustrated by Nancy Grossman. New
York: Holt, Rinehart & Winston, 1967.
HUNT, IRENE. *Across Five Aprils.* Illustrated by Albert John Pucci. Chicago:
Follett Publishing Co., 1964.
LENSKI, LOIS. *High-Rise Secret.* Philadelphia: J. B. Lippincott Co., 1966.
McCLOSKEY, ROBERT. *Homer Price.* New York: Viking Press, 1943.
MERRILL, JEAN. *The Pushcart War.* Illustrated by Ronni Solbert. New York:
William R. Scott, 1964.
NESS, EVALINE. *Sam, Bangs and Moonshine.* New York: Holt, Rinehart &
Winston, 1966.
NEVILLE, EMILY. *Berries Goodman.* New York: Harper & Row, 1965.
———. *The Seventeenth-Street Gang.* New York: Harper & Row, 1966.
NORTON, MARY. *The Borrowers.* New York: Harcourt, Brace & World, 1953.
O'DELL, SCOTT. *Island of the Blue Dolphins.* Boston: Houghton Mifflin Co.,
1960.
POTTER, BEATRIX. *The Tale of Peter Rabbit.* New York: Frederick Warne &
Co., 1901.
SCOTT, ANN HERBERT. *Sam.* Illustrated by Symeon Shimin. New York:
McGraw-Hill Book Co., 1967.
SENDAK, MAURICE. *Where the Wild Things Are.* New York: Harper & Row,
1963.
SEYMOUR, ALTA HALVERSON. *Toward Morning.* Chicago: Follett Publishing
Co., 1961.

SHOTWELL, LOUISA. *Roosevelt Grady*. Illustrated by Peter Burchard. New York: World Publishing Co., 1963.

SORENSON, VIRGINIA. *Plain Girl*. New York: Harcourt, Brace & World, 1955.

SPERRY, ARMSTRONG. *Call It Courage*. New York: Macmillan Co., 1940.

STEELE, WILLIAM O. *The Perilous Road*. Illustrated by Paul Galdone. New York: Harcourt, Brace & World, 1958.

STEPTOE, JOHN. *Stevie*. New York: Harper & Row, 1969.

TWAIN, MARK. *Adventures of Huckleberry Finn*. New York: Harper & Row, 1884, 1931.

WEIK, MARY HAYS. *The Jazz Man*. Illustrated by Ann Grifalconi. New York: Atheneum Publishers, 1966.

WHITE, E. B. *Stuart Little*. New York: Harper & Row, 1945.

————. *Charlotte's Web*. Illustrated by Garth Williams. New York: Harper & Row, 1952.

WOJCIECHOWSKA, MAIA. *Shadow of A Bull*. New York: Atheneum Publishers, 1964.

YATES, ELIZABETH. *Someday You'll Write*. New York: E. P. Dutton & Co., 1962.

chapter 4

literary style
in narrative fiction

The critic of children's literature is concerned not only with literary form and elements, but also with the selection and ordering of the language in children's books. Language is the medium through which literature is expressed; it shapes literature by its possibilities and its limitations and, conversely, literature shapes language. In order to interpret literature fully, the critical reader should be able to recognize *how* language contributes to meaning through analyzing the author's manipulation of it. W. H. Auden sees language as a verbal contraption and says readers should see how it works.

Literary analysis is not simply picking a work apart; rather, it involves a sensitive recognition of what makes a piece of writing effective. Moreover, the intent of analysis is not merely to define the language of literature, but to be aware of what one is experiencing. The purpose of careful reading is to obtain the total meaning of a work, and this cannot be done by looking at separate elements. The language images, ideas, and rhythms must be examined in relation to all other elements for they are not separate parts of meaning; they shape the meaning. Language used with force and vitality does not just tell about life— life *radiates* from it. As an author takes deliberate control of language to create worlds, to relate incidents, to reveal characters, to invent symbols, and to illustrate theme, the critic should reflect upon what is occurring.

Wellek and Warren describe four perspectives from which styles can be examined:

> According to the relations of words to the object, styles are divisible into conceptual and sensuous, succinct and long-winded, or minimizing and exaggerating, decisive and vague, quiet and excited, low and high, simple and decorated; according to the relations among the words, into tense and lax, plastic and musical, smooth and rough, colorless and colorful; according to the relations of words to the total

system of the language, into spoken and written, cliché and individual; and according to the relation of the words to the author, into objective and subjective.[1]

They proceed to describe two methods for approaching a stylistic analysis. The first involves a systematic analysis of the work's linguistic system, interpreting its features in terms of the aesthetic purpose as "total meaning." Their second approach is to study the sum of individual traits by which this system differs from comparable systems. Using this method of contrast, the critic might note the deviations from normal usage and thus discern aesthetic purpose. They suggest a procedure for accomplishing this task.

> In ordinary communicative speech, no attention is drawn to the sound of words, or to word order (which, in English at least, will normally pass from actor to action), or to sentence structure (which will be enumerative, coordinate). A first step in stylistic analysis will be to observe such deviations as the repetitions of sound, the inversion of word order, the construction of involved hierarchies of clauses, all of which must serve some aesthetic function. . . .[2]

The two-phased analysis requires looking at the internal linguistic structure of the work and at the external relationship of its system to others. Examining the text carefully is necessary in order to obtain the total meaning inherent in the work; comparing it with other works helps to identify its unique features. The linguistic features of the individual work could be examined from phonological, syntactical, and semantic perspectives. The features elicited by these analyses, viewed in relation to the total meaning of the work, could be contrasted with other works of the same genre, or with ones portraying a similar theme.

Many people have experiences similar to ones about which they read, but an artist with words casts familiar events into a framework that gives them entirely new dimensions. Furthermore, the skilled author makes it appear that the story tells itself; he does not interfere to point out what happened or to tell the reader how to react. He lets the reader *see* what happened in the dialogue, the action, and in the character's thoughts. Having an experience about which to write may be a prerequisite to a good story, but control of language is vitally more important. David Daiches puts it well.

> To achieve the illusion of a living and pulsing world is not the work of the man who merely knows life and feels strongly about it; it is the work of the writer who can handle language in such a way that

---

[1]René Wellek and Austin Warren, *Theory of Literature*, 3d ed. (New York: Harcourt, Brace & World, 1956), p. 179. Copyright © 1956 by Harcourt, Brace & World, Inc. and reprinted with their permission.

[2]Ibid., p. 180.

what he knows and feels can be carried alive into the reader's imagination.[3]

When an author captures the essence of life in his language, his choice of words and style seem to belong to his subject and the chosen literary form. Appropriate language appears to be a natural part of the story to be told and is not forced. May Hill Arbuthnot says that words, fraught with meaning, should also fall felicitously on the ear and read aloud comfortably and pleasantly.[4] Although the naturalness and the truly artistic elements of eloquent writing remain the province of the artist, the reader can recognize some of the techniques he employs in his creation.

Language Manipulation for Aesthetic Purposes

An author has an infinite number of stylistic choices available for every image, idea, or emotion he wants to relay. The choices he makes determine his style and provide the means of communication with his readers. Whether or not the reader obtains the meaning the author has transmitted depends somewhat upon the style and somewhat upon the language competence of the reader. Readers need to be aware of increasingly complex levels of abstraction in order to experience the full range of meaning in literature. From understanding the simplest level of sign, referent, and denotative meanings, the critic of children's literature comes to recognize descriptive passages, connotative meanings, double meanings, imagery, metaphorical usage, symbolism, allusions, and irony. Beyond the word meanings, he needs to be sensitive to sentence rhythms, features of sound, word order, and the effects of point of view. Some techniques of style are dictated by conventions of the form chosen; others are determined by the personal taste and skill of the author. There may never be a system for complete understanding of all the nuances of language, but the following sections illustrate some variations that occur when language is manipulated consciously for special effect.

DENOTATION AND CONNOTATION

Authors use denotative meanings to tell their stories and to play against, for these are the dictionary meanings of words—they are the

---

[3]David Daiches, "The Criticism of Fiction: Some Second Thoughts." In *Literary Essays*, 1956. Reprinted here with permission of Oliver & Boyd, Edinburgh. Also reprinted in *An Introduction to Literary Criticism*, Marlies Danziger and W. Stacy Johnson, ed., p. 343. Copyright © 1961 by D. C. Heath & Co., Lexington, Mass.

[4]May Hill Arbuthnot, *Children and Books*, 3d ed. (Chicago: Scott Foresman & Co., 1964), p. 18.

generally agreed-upon meanings in language community. Connotation is all that a word brings to mind or suggests; it involves implications, inferences, and associations. Ability to recognize the connotative meanings is necessary for a reader to go beyond the literal level and is required for reading literature of merit. Simple descriptions, understatement, and implied meanings require comprehension at both literal and interpretative levels. In one of Barbara Picard's excellent novels set in historical times, the reader must go beyond the literal level to grasp the full meaning in this event. Sir Ralf has taken the wandering Lost John as his squire, when his own son, Alain, who is John's age, returns from a monastery in which he had been studying.

> Holding Midnight's bridle, with all the eagerness and bustle of armed men about him, John felt a lump in his throat. With his head turned away, he said, 'You'll . . . you'll take care, will you not, sir? Please.'
> Sir Ralf placed a hand on each of John's shoulders and turned him so that he was forced to look at him. 'I shall take care, never

Illustration by Charles Keeping, from Barbara Leonie Picard's *Lost John*. Copyright © 1963 by Oxford University Press and reproduced with their permission.

fear.' He laughed and clapped John on the shoulder. 'And mind you keep out of mischief while I'm gone.' And then, as though John had really been his own son, he kissed him before turning to mount Midnight.

Alain, watching them from the doorway of the kitchen, a dull ache at his heart, wished he did not love his father quite so much.[5]

Picard *shows* instead of tells and has her characters act out the emotions in the scene. She creates the conditions for the reader to identify with the characters and to discover affective meanings by using both denotative and connotative meanings of words.

Authors play with language in telling stories, and their word games delight those who understand the double meanings and puns. Lewis Carroll's clever language appeals to adults as well as to children because it can be read for several layers of meaning. Less complex than the absurdities, rhymes, and strange characters used by Carroll are the word games played by Roald Dahl. His creation, Mr. Willy Wonka, is taking a group of children through his chocolate factory.

They passed a yellow door on which it said: STOREROOM NUM-BER 77—ALL THE BEANS, CACAO BEANS, COFFEE BEANS, JELLY BEANS, AND HAS BEANS.

"Has beans?" cried Violet Beauregarde.

"You're one yourself!" said Mr. Wonka. "There's no time for arguing! Press on, press on!"[6]

In this book, as in many fantasies, the words can be read at one level for enjoyment, and at a deeper level for further understandings. A similar book published earlier, and equally popular with children, is *The Phantom Tollbooth*.[7] The play on words is heavy, but children who recognize the double entendres appreciate the humor. In this book, subtraction stew served by the Mathemagician increased hunger, and a banquet was held in which everyone had to eat his words.

Wellek and Warren speak of poetry, but their observation applies to prose, as well.

. . . the line-ends of verses, the grouping into stanzas, the paragraphs of prose passages, eye-rhymes or puns which are comprehensible only through spelling, and many similar devices must be considered integral factors of literary works of art.[8]

[5]Barbara Leonie Picard, *Lost John*, illustrated by Charles Keeping (New York: Criterion Books, 1963), pp. 109-110.

[6]Roald Dahl, *Charlie and the Chocolate Factory*, illustrated by Joseph Schindelman (New York: Alfred A. Knopf, 1964), p. 92.

[7]Norton Juster, *The Phantom Tollbooth*, illustrated by Jules Feiffer (New York: Random House, 1961).

[8]Wellek and Warren, *Theory of Literature*, p. 144.

The semantic analysis of the linguistic system in a literary work will reveal the author's amusement with language.

Some authors play word games as a way of naming their characters, and some use names to describe the nature of the characterization. Carol Kendall uses names such as Muggles, Gummy, Curley Green, Mingy, and Walter the Earl to reveal something about the characters in *The Gammage Cup.*[9] Tove Jansson uses names such as Snufkin, Teetywoo, Gaffsie, My, Snork Maiden, and Sniff, and words such as the hatti-fatteners, a fillyjonk, and a whomper, to add to the delight and humor of the Moomin tales.[10] James Thurber uses double-talk, among other things, to put across his humor.

> If you can touch the clocks and never start them, then you can start the clocks and never touch them. That's logic, as I know and use it.[11]

Word play includes a child in the joke, and lets him realize that language is beautiful but slippery; it can twist meaning with its surprises and delights.

IRONY AND HUMOR

Irony depends upon incongruous comparisons used intentionally to create a feeling of conflict. Satire, as one form of irony, appears for diverse purposes in children's literature. It is used to create humor, and it is used as bitter commentary on social customs. In this excerpt, it is both. Portman, the largest mouse, had called a meeting:

> "Therefore," said Portman in a deep squeak, "your Steering Committee has come up with a solution."
> "What's a Steering Committee?" said Asa, one of the two smallest mice, to his brother, Rambo, the other smallest mouse.
> "It's Portman and his friends deciding before the meeting starts what we're going to decide in the meeting," said Rambo.
> "Is that fair?" said Asa.
> "It's customary," said Rambo.[12]

FIGURATIVE LANGUAGE

Figurative language is a term used to encompass all types of writing that signify more than denotative meanings. Literal understanding is

---

[9]Carol Kendall, *The Gammage Cup,* illustrated by Erik Blegvad (New York: Harcourt, Brace & World, 1959).

[10]Tove Jansson, *Tales from Moominvalley* (New York: Henry Z. Walck, 1964).

[11]James Thurber, *The Thirteen Clocks,* illustrated by Marc Simont (New York: Simon & Schuster, 1950), p. 106. Copyright © 1950 by James Thurber.

[12]Mary Stolz, *Belling the Tiger,* illustrated by Beni Montresor (New York: Harper & Row, 1961), p. 11. Copyright © 1961 by Mary Stolz. Reprinted with permission of Harper & Row, Publishers.

obtained from denotative meanings, but the language of literature carries deeper meaning. Words used metaphorically attempt to describe one thing in terms normally denoting another; thus, a mulish boy, a thunderous voice, a kittenish girl. Figurative language is filled with analogies and is intended to call forth mental images, connotations, and symbolic meanings. Metaphors are stated comparisons intended to evoke mental images, such as Lionni's lobster who walked about like a water-moving machine.[13] Mental images have powerful emotional qualities, and so metaphors are closely linked with the mood or emotional context of a passage.

The infinite number of choices available in figurative language gives the creative mind great freedom of expression, although two cautions are appropriate for children's literature; one is that flowery and elaborate language can interfere with understanding, and the other is the need for referents to be familiar to children. Bushes that look like popcorn balls and cars that look like big, fat raisins are more likely to be meaningful to children than skin like monumental alabaster. Figurative language takes many forms, such as the metaphors mentioned, but it can also be personification, allusions, symbolism, similes, allegories, and imagery. Some of the forms are illustrated below.

Imagery. Literary language differs from scientific language in many ways. One major source of distinction is in the use of imagery—word pictures which are developed by metaphors, similes, allusions, and tropes. Although it appears more in poetry than in prose, imagery is an attempt to exploit the resources of language deliberately and systematically through direct sense appeal and through figures of speech combining two or more elements. A consistent pattern of imagery can become symbolism, but imagery is used primarily for describing and establishing mood. The differences between imagery and symbolism are illustrated in *The Cabin Faced West*. Ann Hamilton, the central figure, looks longingly at her blue shoes and her mother's china plates because they represent all the elegant things she remembered from her life in Gettysburg before her family moved west. The shoes and the china help the reader to picture mentally the life she loved back in Gettysburg. Ann goes frequently to the road to sit, and this becomes symbolic in the story. But the road signifies more than the way back to Gettysburg.

> Of all the places on her father's hill, Ann liked the road best. Sometimes her mother said she had a "feeling in her bones." She couldn't

---

[13]Leo Lionni, *Swimmy* (New York: Pantheon Books, 1963), unpaged.

explain it; it was just there. That was the way Ann was about the road.[14]

Imagery is a subtle element in narrative fiction; it forms a pattern below the level of plot and character. Images give tone to writing style and help an author establish a mood. Lloyd Alexander uses metaphorical devices of language to extend characterization in a series of books, one of which was awarded the Newbery Medal. In the first of the series, *The Book of Three,* each of Taran's companions uses a figure of speech that becomes an extension of his personality. Eilonwy uses similes and metaphors.

> On not knowing someone's name she says it makes her feel "wrong footed . . . as if I had three thumbs on one hand . . . It's clumsy." (p. 69).
>
> On vexing people on purpose, "It's like handing them a toad." (p. 79).
>
> On crying, "It makes my nose feel like a melted icicle." (p. 96).
>
> On stroking a fawn, "It makes you feel all tingly, as if you were touching the wind." (p. 139).
>
> On people who say I told you so, "That's worse than somebody coming up and eating your dinner before you have a chance to sit down." (p. 187).
>
> On watching someone sleep, "It's like counting stones in a wall." (p. 200).[15]

Allusions. Allusions are implied or indirect references to a Biblical, literary, or historical person, object, or idea that an author wants to associate with a situation he is describing. It is intended to bring to the current situation the heritage of feeling associated with the reference. Allusions are effective devices when the reader is familiar with the subject alluded to, and very subtle allusions are possible when a group has a large common literary heritage. Most allusions in children's literature refer to the myths, such as Achilles' heel, a Midas touch, the wings of Pegasus. Authors of children's books reveal their own literary backgrounds through the use of allusions, as Madeleine L'Engle does in *A Wrinkle in Time*[16] and in the Austin series.[17]

Symbolism and Allegory. A symbol is a visible sign of something invisible, such as abstract ideas, emotions, or personality characteristics

---

[14]Jean Fritz, *The Cabin Faced West,* illustrated by Feodor Rojankovsky (New York: Coward-McCann, 1958), pp. 14-15. Copyright © 1958 by Jean Fritz. Reprinted with permission of Coward-McCann, Inc.

[15]Lloyd Alexander, *The Book of Three,* illustrated by Evaline Ness (New York: Holt, Rinehart & Winston, 1964).

[16]Madeleine L'Engle, *A Wrinkle in Time* (New York: Farrar, Straus & Giroux, 1962).

[17]Madeleine L'Engle, *Meet the Austins* (New York: Vanguard Press, 1961).

which may be represented by an object, a character, a setting, or a total work that suggests a meaning larger than its literal self. Although symbols are intended to add dimensions to literature, and recognition of them provides a deeper meaning than accepting them literally, they can never be fully explained. Symbols resist total explanation for they suggest, reveal, and conceal all at the same time. Brooks and Warren point out that there are some symbols recognized widely and some used in very particular contexts.

> The crown, like the cross and the flag, is a conventional symbol. That is, men have agreed that the figure of the cross should stand for Christianity, that a flag of a certain design should stand for the United States of America, and that the circlet of gold should stand for the power and authority of kingship. Such conventional symbols occur in literature just as they occur in our daily speech, but the symbolism with which we are characteristically concerned as we read poems and stories is not conventional. It is special and is related to a particular context. . . . In literature, objects and events often become symbolic, possessing a wider significance and thus becoming expressive of the author's meaning. Since fiction is concrete and dramatic in its presentation, the author must necessarily make use of symbols at some level; for he does not "state" his meanings abstractly but renders them through the presentation of concrete particulars.[18]

Symbols are found in nearly every literary genre. Characters are symbolic in much folk literature, as they sometimes are in modern realism and fantasy. Objects or settings are used as symbols, such as the broom in *Hurry Home, Candy*,[19] or the neat and orderly house of Mr. Kobalt in *Dorp Dead*.[20] A dog's bellowing voice is used symbolically in *Sounder*.[21]

The many levels of figurative language could be arranged in an hierarchical order to illustrate the levels of abstraction. One attempt to show that image, metaphor, symbol, and myth are increasingly complex instances of the same phenomena requires an entire chapter in Wellek and Warren. The following excerpt illustrates the relationship:

> Is there any important sense in which "symbol" differs from "image" and "metaphor"? Primarily, we think, in the recurrence and per-

---

18Cleanth Brooks and Robert Penn Warren, *Understanding Fiction*, 2d ed. (New York: Appleton-Century-Crofts, 1959), p. 74. Copyright © 1959 by Educational Division, Meredith Corp. Reprinted with permission of Appleton-Century-Crofts.

19Meindert DeJong, *Hurry Home, Candy*, illustrated by Maurice Sendak (New York: Harper & Row, 1953).

20Julia Cunningham, *Dorp Dead*, illustrated by James Spanfeller (New York: Pantheon Books, 1965).

21William H. Armstrong, *Sounder*, illustrated by James Barkley (New York: Harper & Row, 1969).

sistence of the "symbol." An "image" may be invoked once as a metaphor, but if it persistently recurs, both as presentation and representation, it becomes a symbol, may even become part of a symbolic (or mythic) system.[22]

The extended use of symbols becomes a mythic system, or as illustrated in children's literature, it becomes an allegory. In an allegory, each character and element is more important as a symbol than it is as its literal self. Meanings are made even more abstract by interaction among the symbols. Concepts of good and evil are personified in *The Lion, the Witch, and the Wardrobe*[23] where each character represents something beyond himself. Since C. S. Lewis was a theologian, it is understandable that there should be strong religious parallels in the Narnia series.

The Animal Family[24] by Jarrell, *Dorp Dead*[25] by Cunningham, and *A Wrinkle in Time*[26] by L'Engle are each allegories. The characters in *The Animal Family* suggest that a family can be any assortment of human and nonhuman beings, with the important criteria being the feeling of love and familyness. Gilly Ground in *Dorp Dead* represents the human need to be loved and respected as an individual. And Meg shows her love can overcome the powerful force of evil in "It" in *A Wrinkle in Time.*

Authors are asked to explain the symbolic or hidden meanings in stories or poems, but as Ciardi illustrates in *How Does a Poem Mean?*,[27] they really cannot do it. Cunningham was asked to explain the character, the Hunter, in *Dorp Dead*. Here is her comment:

> I have been asked to explain the Hunter. Was he meant to be a symbol of Christ or at least of Christ's goodness? Maybe. I do not know. I think the Hunter is no more or less than that person or, if one is lucky, persons who pass through every life for a moment, or sometimes longer, and give it strength and meaning. Why didn't he have a name? I guess I did not give him a name because he has so many.[28]

Enriched experiences with literature are possible when the deeper significance in language is recognized and, although symbol mongers

[22]Wellek and Warren, *Theory of Literature*, p. 189.

[23]C. S. Lewis, *The Lion, the Witch, and the Wardrobe*, illustrated by Pauline Baynes (New York: Macmillan Co., 1950, 1961).

[24]Randall Jarrell, *The Animal Family*, illustrated by Maurice Sendak (New York: Pantheon Books, 1965).

[25]Julia Cunningham, *Dorp Dead*.

[26]Madeleine L'Engle, *A Wrinkle in Time*.

[27]John Ciardi, *How Does a Poem Mean?* (Boston: Houghton Mifflin Co., 1959).

[28]Julia Cunningham, "Dear Characters," *The Horn Book Magazine*, vol. 43, (April, 1967), pp. 233-234. Copyright © 1967 by the Horn Book, Inc. Reprinted with permission of The Horn Book, Inc.

are not the goal of literature instruction, complete understanding of a piece of literature is desirable. Children's literature differs from adult literature quantitatively rather than qualitatively, and those who read it at a surface level miss its richness.

Point of View

The point of view from which a story is told is a primary determinant of literary style; its choice affects the language, the signs of authenticity, and the feelings of intimacy achieved in the narrative. Brooks and Warren prefer a more precise statement about the focus of narration, which they describe below.

> . . . the focus of narration has to do with who tells the story. We may make four basic distinctions: (1) a character may tell his own story in the first person; (2) a character may tell, in the first person, a story which he has observed; (3) the author may tell what happens in the purely objective sense—deeds, words, gestures—without going into the minds of the characters and without giving his own comment; (4) the author may tell what happens with full liberty to go into the minds of characters and to give his own comment. These four types of narration may be called: (1) first-person, (2) first-person observer, (3) author-observer, and (4) omniscient author. Combinations of these methods are, of course, possible.[29]

Authors of children's literature use all four vantage points. The once maligned first person narrative is used increasingly with evident success, although it does restrict what the author is able to reveal; every thing is filtered through the sensory perceptions of the narrator. This focal point provides a feeling of intimacy with the narrator, usually the central character, and it also provides a means of identification with him, one that is rarely as intense from other points of view. The language of the entire narrative is written in the voice of the narrator, as illustrated in *Stevie*.

> And on Saturdays when his mother comes to pick him up, he always tries to act cute just cause his mother is there.
> He picked up my airplane and I told him not to bother it.
> He thought I wouldn't say nothin' to him in front of his mother.
> I could never go anywhere without my mother sayin' "Take Stevie with you now."
> "But why I gotta take him everywhere I go?" I'd say.
> "Now if you were stayin' with someone you wouldn't want them to treat you mean," my mother told me.
> "Why don't you and Stevie try to play nice?"

---

[29]Brooks and Warren, *Understanding Fiction*, p. 684.

Illustration by John Steptoe, from his book, *Stevie*. Copyright © 1969 by John Steptoe. Used by permission of Harper & Row, Publishers.

Yeah, but I always been nice to him with his old spoiled self.
He's always gotta have his way anyway.[30]

Since *Stevie* is told in the first person, it is appropriate that the narration between the dialogue is written in the same authentic speech patterns exhibited in the conversations.

Paul Zindel creates a unique set of circumstances by using two voices, each in the first person, to tell the story of *The Pigman*. John and Lorraine tell alternate chapters in the book, each from his own point of view. John speaks.

Now, I don't like school, which you might say is one of the factors that got us involved with this old guy we nicknamed the Pigman. Actually, I hate school, but then again most of the time I hate everything.

Then Lorraine.

I should never have let John write the first chapter because he always has to twist things subliminally. I am not panting, and I'm not about to have a thrombosis. It's just that some very strange things have happened to us during the last few months, and we feel we should write them down while they're still fresh in our minds. It's got to be written now before John and I mature and repress the the whole thing.[31]

John and Lorraine reveal themselves through the narration; they illustrate the dreariness of their existence, and the hopelessness of trying to communicate with their parents. They also reveal their tragic flaw; they are still childlike and do not think of the consequences of their actions. A similar age group is represented in *The Dream Watcher,* with its attendant jargon of the day, but only one boy speaks here.

I'd better begin this story by telling you that until a month ago I was quite a mess. I mean, I was such a mess that my mother wanted to send me to a psychiatrist but backed down when she discovered that it would cost twenty-five dollars an hour. Twenty-five dollars an hour was too much even for her.[32]

The use of the voice, as represented here, brings a sense of immediacy and intimacy to the reader. Many children are able to identify with the characters, helped not only by the similarity of circumstances in their lives, but also by the use of the pronoun "I."

---

[30]John Steptoe, *Stevie*, illustrated by John Steptoe (New York: Harper & Row, 1969), unpaged. Copyright © 1969 by John L. Steptoe. Reprinted with permission of Harper & Row, Publishers.
[31]Paul Zindel, *The Pigman* (New York: Harper & Row, 1968), pp. 1 and 7. Copyright © by Paul Zindel. Reprinted with permission of Harper & Row, Publishers.
[32]Barbara Wersba, *The Dream Watcher* (New York: Atheneum Publishers, 1968), p. 3. Copyright © 1968 by Barbara Wersba. Used by permission of Atheneum Publishers, and McIntosh and Otis, Inc.

Younger children will be able to identify with Mark, who tells his story in *About the B'Nai Bagels*. Mark's language is flavored with the idiom of American Jewish families, and his major problem centers in his doting mother. Mark notes that his mother takes the role of motherhood seriously; she plays the role of martyr with a good amount of zest. He comments on her concern with keeping him well fed.

> In fact, if my mother could rewrite the Ten Commandments, one of them would be "thou shalt eateth of breakfast."

Mark's mother comments to her sister about her son's disregard for appropriate dress.

> "Better that he would wear sneakers to synagogue on Saturday morning, Thelma, than that he shouldn't go at all."[33]

Just as Mark's voice reflects the culture in which his story is set, so Miguel's voice reflects the culture of his primitive Mexican village. His language—his manner of speech—has a distinct Spanish flavor as he says:

> I am Miguel. For most people it does not make so much difference that I am Miguel. But for me, often, it is a very great trouble.[34]

Authenticity of character and setting is increased by the consistency in speech and tone of narrative fiction. Authors of historical fiction face a particular problem of keeping the language and forms of speech appropriate to the period, as well as of maintaining accuracy in other details. The Beattys describe the problem of writing historical fiction in the first person.

> A first-person novel presented a problem which we had completely overlooked. The book was not simply a novel—it was also a journal! We had been careful to keep the conversations on an accurate seventeenth century level, but we had neglected the narrative, which in a first-person book *also* had to be couched in the speech of 1651.[35]

Patricia Clapp dealt with a similar problem in *Constance*,[36] for her novel was recorded as a diary by her central character.

The point of view chosen, the literary form, and the setting combine to affect the literary style of the narrative. Whereas the Beattys

---

[33]Elaine L. Konigsburg, *About the B'Nai Bagels* (New York: Atheneum Publishers, 1969), pp. 12-13, p. 68. Copyright © 1969 by E. L. Konigsburg. Used by permission of Atheneum Publishers.

[34]Joseph Krumgold, *. . . And Now Miguel*, illustrated by Jean Charlot (New York: Thomas Y. Crowell Co., 1953), p. 1. Copyright © 1953 by Joseph Krumgold. Reprinted by permission of Thomas Y. Crowell Co., Inc.

[35]John and Patricia Beatty, "Watch Your Language—You're Writing for Young People!" *The Horn Book Magazine*, vol. 41, February 1965, p. 34. Copyright © 1965 by The Horn Book, Inc. Reprinted with permission of The Horn Book, Inc.

[36]Patricia Clapp, *Constance: A Story of Early Plymouth* (New York: Lothrop, Lee & Shepard Co., 1968).

faced a language problem because they chose to write historical fiction in the first person, deAngeli faced a similar challenge, for her story is set in medieval times. In *The Door in the Wall,* both the narrative and the dialogue are written in a style appropriate to the medieval period in history. Robin is angered when he is unable to handle a chisel; he throws it away.

> "Treacherous misguided tool!" he shouted. "I'll have no more of you!"
> Brother Matthew looked up in astonishment. "Tis not the tool that is at fault, but thine unskilled hands," he said quietly.
> "If thou'rt to learn to use it, patience and care are better teachers than a bad temper."
> "Think you I am but a carpenter's son and apprentice?"[37]

Another author, writing in the third person, added to the authenticity of the setting by the use of language in *Roosevelt Grady.* The Appalachian dialect and speech patterns appear in the narrative as well as in the dialogue.

> The Opportunity Class. That's where the bean-pickers got put.
> Roosevelt Grady wondered what it meant.
> Roosevelt knew about schools. Third grade, fourth grade, things like that. He knew about schools from experience: three weeks here, six weeks there, a day or two somewhere else. But Opportunity Class. This was something new.
>
> . . . .
>
> He was sick and tired of taking away. He wanted to learn about putting into.
> At the last school where he'd been, they'd finished taking away and begun on putting into. That he liked. Being there when they began on something new made him feel regular, as though he belonged. Besides, putting into had one special thing about it he purely had to find out.[38]

Authentic speech is demanded by the first person point of view; it may also be demanded by the literary form. Since folktales mirror the speech and customs of the people, the language used to tell them is colloquial. In *The Jack Tales*[39] and *The Grandfather Tales,*[40] the language is written in the dialect of the mountain people who told the tales. Phrases such as "a right smart distance," "fix up and go back,"

---

[37]Marguerite deAngeli, *The Door in the Wall* (Garden City, N. Y.: Doubleday & Co., 1949), p. 28. Copyright © 1949 by Marguerite deAngeli. Reprinted by permission of Doubleday & Co., Inc.

[38]Reprinted by permission of The World Publishing Co. from *Roosevelt Grady* by Louisa R. Shotwell. Copyright © 1963 by Louisa R. Shotwell.

[39]Richard Chase, ed., *The Jack Tales,* illustrated by Berkeley Williams (Boston: Houghton Mifflin Co., 1943).

[40]Richard Chase, ed., *The Grandfather Tales,* illustrated by Berkeley Williams (Boston: Houghton Mifflin Co., 1948).

and "don't you reckon" illustrate the colloquial speech used in the narrative as well as in the dialogue. Some authors restrict colloquialisms to dialogue and couch the narrative in standard English. Isaac Singer sprinkles the European Jewish folktales with words such as borscht, cheese blintzes, amiable fools of Chelm, guldens, and with characters named Shlemiel and Yenta, but his narrative is in standard English.[41]

Features of Sound

Ordinary prose seldom draws attention to the repetition of speech sounds, but literary prose does so frequently. Some repetitions are obvious as, for instance, alliteration, in which the beginning sound of each word is the same; but most repetitions of sounds are more subtle. In the following E. B. White paragraph, the repeated use of the "s" sound, in addition to the gradual increase in sentence length, adds interest and elegance to the writing.

> The barn was very large. It was very old. It smelled of hay and it smelled of manure. It smelled of the perspiration of tired horses and the wonderful sweet breath of patient cows. It often had a sort of peaceful smell—as though nothing bad could happen ever again in the world. It smelled of grain and of harness dressing and of axle grease and of rubber boots and of new rope. And whenever the cat was given a fish-head to eat, the barn would smell of fish. But mostly it smelled of hay, for there was always hay in the great loft up overhead. And there was always hay being pitched down to the cows and the horses and the sheep.[42]

By concentrating on olfactory sensory images, by gradually increasing the length of sentences, and by repeating sounds, White's paragraph can elicit a vivid mental image for the reader. Phonetic devices, such as repetition, alliteration, and assonance in a rhythmic structure of sentences and paragraphs, reinforce ideas and establish mood.

Repetition of sounds and words is used to heighten the drama of action or the characterization in a story. Milne's use of repetition reveals the nature of Pooh's character and adds a lyric quality to the prose as Pooh reasons deductively:

> That buzzing-noise means something. You don't get a buzzing-noise like that, just buzzing and buzzing, without its meaning something. If there's a buzzing-noise, somebody's making a buzzing-noise, and

---

[41]Isaac Bashevis Singer, *Zlateh the Goat and Other Stories,* illustrated by Maurice Sendak (New York: Harper & Row, 1966).

[42]E. B. White, *Charlotte's Web,* illustrated by Garth Williams (New York: Harper & Row, 1952), p. 13. Copyright © 1952 by E. B. White. Reprinted with permission of Harper & Row, Publishers.

the only reason for making a buzzing-noise that I know of is because you're a bee.[43]

Other authors use repetition of words and sentence patterns to involve the reader in the pathos or to engage him in the trauma of a story. DeJong does it in *Hurry Home, Candy*.

> The dog had no name. For a dog to have a name, someone must have him and someone must love him, and a dog must have someone. The dog had no one, and no one had the dog. The dog had only the silent empty countryside of the few houses. The dog had only the crumbs and cleaned bones he could pick up at the few houses. The dog had only himself, so the dog had nothing, and he was afraid.[44]

DeJong portrays a dog's reaction without resorting to use of word images, and the animals in his books communicate on a purely instinctive level. His stories, with many set in Holland, display DeJong's skill with language, whether the stories be about animals or about children. The language in *Journey from Peppermint Street* reveals DeJong's sensitivity and perceptiveness, and in the following excerpt, he again uses repetition of sounds. Aunt Hinka had substituted a tile for her hand on Siebren's back when he was supposed to be going to sleep.

> Something in you knew it was meant to be kind, but that didn't help the part that knew it was to fool you. Siebren lay, trying not to breathe, trying to be so rigidly still that when the uncle did come, he'd think Siebren was dead. But still the part that couldn't believe Aunt Hinka was scrunched in the farthest cold corner of the great stone room—was squeezed in the corner, screaming with horror.[45]

Children respond to the rhythm, rhyme, and repetition of Kipling's *Just So Stories*, particularly *The Elephant's Child*.

> So he said good-by very politely to the Bi-Colored-Python-Rock-Snake, and helped to coil him up on the rock again, and went on, a little warm but not at all astonished, eating melons and throwing the rind about till he trod on what he thought was a log at the very edge of the great, gray-green, greasy Limpopo River all set about with fever-trees. But it was really the Crocodile, oh Best Beloved, and the Crocodile winked one eye.[46]

---

[43]A. A. Milne, *Winnie-the-Pooh*, illustrated by Ernest H. Shepard (New York: E. P. Dutton & Co., 1926), p. 4. Copyright © 1926 by E. P. Dutton & Co., Inc. Renewal 1954 by A. A. Milne. Reprinted by permission of the publishers.

[44]Meindert DeJong, *Hurry Home, Candy* (New York: Harper & Row, 1953), p. 3. Copyright © 1953 by Meindert DeJong. Reprinted with permission of Harper & Row, Publishers.

[45]Meindert DeJong, *Journey from Peppermint Street*, illustrated by Emily McCully (New York: Harper & Row, 1968), pp. 150-151. Copyright © 1968 by Meindert DeJong. Reprinted with permission of Harper & Row, Publishers.

[46]Rudyard Kipling, *Just So Stories*, pp. 33-34. Reprinted by permission of Mrs. George Bambridge and Doubleday & Company, Inc.

Part of the manipulation of language to achieve special effects is done through repetition of sounds and words. The sense of joy found in reading melodic prose can be extended by recognizing the techniques used to accomplish it.

Syntactic Features of Style

Syntactic patterns, arrangements of words, demonstrate an author's literary style more so than does any other feature. Gleason points out that "Style is the patterning of choices made within the options presented by the conventions of the language and of the literary form."[47] It would appear, then, that syntactic patterns are a means of studying literary styles; however, since the conventions of language allow such a myriad of choices, systematic analyses of style through syntax have been fraught with difficulties. Kellogg Hunt attempted to analyze Faulkner's and Hemingway's styles and proposed the ratio of clause-to-sentence factors as an entering wedge for analysis of literary style.[48] He warned that relying upon merely quantitative data could ignore variations that occur when language is manipulated for special effects. Christensen countered Hunt's approach to defining a mature style by proposing his own measure—a relatively high frequency of free modifiers, especially in the final position, and a relatively high frequency of structures of coordination within the T-unit (Hunt's minimal terminable units).[49] He suggested that a large number of clauses could obfuscate meaning. Michalak holds that transformational analysis describes style better than other methods have done so far.[50] She further states that syntax seems to be the central determinant of style which is a matter not only of the choice of certain structures, but also of their positioning.

Rhythmic prose is a syntactic feature frequently found in children's books. Although the literary value of highly rhythmical prose is questionable, authors use rhythm and repetition to underscore, to unify, to build feeling tone, and to organize speech. Wellek and Warren discuss the organization of speech rhythms.

The artistic rhythm of prose can be described as an organization of ordinary speech rhythms. It differs from ordinary prose by a greater

[47]H. A. Gleason, Jr., *Linguistics and English Grammars* (New York: Holt, Rinehart & Winston, 1965), p. 428.

[48]Kellogg W. Hunt, *Grammatical Structures Written at Three Grade Levels*, NCTE Research Report No. 3 (Champaign, Ill.: National Council of Teachers of English, 1965), p. 70.

[49]Francis Christensen, "Problems of Defining a Mature Style," in *English Journal*, vol. 57, (April, 1968), pp. 572-579.

[50]Joanne Michalak, "The Significance of the 'New' Grammar," in *Emerging Outlines of a New Rhetoric* (Oshkosh, Wis.: Wisconsin Council of Teachers of English, 1966), pp. 39-45.

regularity of stress distribution, which, however, must not reach an apparent isochronism (that is, a regularity of time intervals between rhythmical accents). In an ordinary sentence there are usually considerable differences of intensity and pitch, while in rhythmical prose there is a marked tendency toward a leveling of stress and pitch differences. . . . There are all kinds of gradations from almost non-rhythmical prose: from chopped sentences full of accumulated stresses to rhythmical prose approaching the regularity of verse.[51]

Children seem to have a natural sense of rhythm and are frequently drawn to literature because of its rhythmic language. Rhythm and rhyme are used in a very obvious way in the works of Seuss, Bemelmans, and de Regniers.

By the light of the moon, by the light of a star,
they walked all night from near to far.[52]

Madeline soon ate and drank. On her bed there was a crank. And a crack on the ceiling had the habit of sometimes looking like a rabbit.[53]

I told the Queen and the Queen told the King,
I had a friend I wanted to bring.[54]

Authors manipulate rhythm in sentence patterns to achieve an aesthetic purpose, to clarify meaning, and to establish a mood. Short staccato sentences build feelings of tenseness; long rambling ones contribute to an ethereal mood. In the following excerpt from *Sounder,* Armstrong achieves a contrast of tension and restraint partially by varying the pattern of sentence rhythms. The boy had taken a cake to his father in jail, and a deputy sheriff had torn it to shreds looking for a file or hacksaw blade inside it.

The man shoved the box into the boy's hands and swore again. Part of the cake fell to the floor; it was only a box of crumbs now. The man swore again and made the boy pick up the crumbs from the floor.
The boy hated the man with the red face with the same total but helpless hatred he had felt when he saw his father chained, when he saw Sounder shot. He had thought how he would like to chain the deputy sheriff behind his own wagon and then scare the horse so that it would run faster than the cruel man could. The deputy would fall and bounce and drag on the frozen road. His fine leather jacket would be torn more than he had torn his father's

[51]Wellek and Warren, *Theory of Literature,* pp. 164-165.
[52]Dr. Seuss (Theodore Seuss Geisel), *One Fish, Two Fish, Red Fish, Blue Fish* (New York: Random House, 1959), unpaged.
[53]Ludwig Bemelmans, *Madeline* (New York: Viking Press, 1939), unpaged.
[54]Beatrice Schenk de Regniers, *May I Bring a Friend?*, illustrated by Beni Montresor (New York: Atheneum Publishers, 1964), unpaged. Copyright © 1964 by Beatrice de Regniers. Used by permission of Atheneum Publishers.

Illustration by James Barkley, from William H. Armstrong's *Sounder*. Copyright © 1969 by James Barkley. Used by permission of Harper & Row, Publishers.

overalls. He would yell and curse, and that would make the horse go faster. And the boy would just watch, not trying to stop the wagon. . . .[55]

Armstrong's long phrases are contrasted with the staccato-like ones to create a feeling of tenseness. He contrasts several one-syllable verbs, such as shoved, swore, fall, bounce, drag, yell, and curse, with a suddenly passive phrase, "And the boy would just watch." The strong emotions of the boy penetrate the language, but his control and restraint are revealed with equal strength. A mythic quality permeates the story, as the human characters are known only as the boy, the man, the deputy, and the father. This author is aware of the effect of using the best words in the best order to contain the essence of life.

Helen Buckley manipulates sentence rhythms to portray the feelings of a child who must hurry when he is with Mother, but who has plenty of time when he is with Grandfather, in *Grandfather and I*.[56] Even the words seem to amble aimlessly, "we can walk along, and walk along, and talk just as long as we please" when the child is with his Grandfather, but when he is with his mother, she walks in a hurry and and talks in a hurry, and she makes him hurry.

A critical reader of literature will be sensitive to the rhythm and beauty of language; he will reject rewritten classics or simplified versions of stories intended to make certain selections available to younger audiences. He will recognize that tampering with the language of the literary piece destroys the integrity of that piece. Words and phrases selected and arranged with an overall purpose in the mind of the author should be allowed to stand immune from well-meaning rewriters.

Summary

Critical analysis reveals how language develops meaning in literature through its various stylistic features. Analysis of style perceives the internal linguistic system of a selection of narrative fiction as well as the relationship of the system to other works. Familiarity with the techniques of style an author employs increases appreciation and heightens the intellectual experience of the reader. Connotations of words help an author to convey meanings and emotions far different from those based on denotative meanings. Humor and social commentary may be derived from irony and satire used by an author. Figurative language

---

[55]William H. Armstrong, *Sounder*, illustrated by James Barkley (New York: Harper & Row, 1969), pp. 59-60. Copyright © 1969 by William H. Armstrong. Reprinted with permission of Harper & Row, Publishers.

[56]Helen E. Buckley, *Grandfather and I*, illustrated by Paul Galdone (New York: Lothrop, Lee & Shepard Co., 1959).

in children's literature is usually constrained by the need for simple referents and directness of imagery. Extension of characterization through metaphor is possible, and effective use of allusion adds meaning to children's literature.

Symbols are sometimes referred to singly, or they can be extended to the level of allegory. Nearly every genre of children's literature evidences some use of symbolism. Examples from contemporary works representing allegory are cited.

The points of view an author chooses determine his mode of communication with the reader and, often, the intensity of the impact of his story. Versatile children's authors improvise within a point of view, and they frequently combine techniques in their narratives.

In writing for children, the important features of sound are employed by authors. Vividness and drama created by artistic use of sound distinguish the quality of writing for children. Similarly, the arrangement of words within sentences or paragraphs, syntactic properties of style, evince interest. Rhythm and repetition are techniques which capture the imagination and the natural impulses of children. The critical reader will be able to identify good writing and to discriminate among children's books by recognizing elements of style.

Activities for Further Study

1. Have students list words with multiple meanings, then use them in sentences that illustrate their different meanings.
2. Read several books with various dialects used in the dialogue. See if children can identify the area from which the characters come (Midwest, the West, the South, Appalachia, French Canada, Washington, D. C., Boston, etc.).
3. Identify the writing style of a particular author. Analyze what he does with language to achieve his unique effect.
4. Find a number of figurative expressions in a piece of fiction. Discuss why they are effective in calling forth mental images, or why they are not.
5. Read a passage that establishes a mood. Identify the words the author used that were helpful in establishing the mood.
6. Have children play word games with you. Start with puns, double meanings, riddles. For example, how do you get down off an elephant? (You don't, you get down from a duck.)
   See Bennett Cerf, *More Riddles,* (New York: Random House, 1961).
   Murray Rockowitz, *Arrow Book of Word Games,* (New York: Scholastic Magazines, 1964).

7. Have students write a paragraph about an incident involving several people. Have them rewrite it from the point of view of each person involved in the incident.

8. Manipulate the syntactic patterns of several sentences. Alter the word order and arrangement of embedded clauses to illustrate the effect on meaning.

Selected References

ALTICK, RICHARD D. *Preface to Critical Reading.* 4th ed. New York: Holt, Rinehart & Winston, 1962.

ARBUTHNOT, MAY HILL. *Children and Books.* 3d ed. Chicago: Scott Foresman & Co., 1964.

BEATTY, JOHN and PATRICIA. "Watch Your Language—You're Writing for Young People!" *The Horn Book Magazine,* vol. 41, February 1965, p. 34.

BROOKS, CLEANTH, and WARREN, ROBERT PENN. *Understanding Fiction.* 2d ed. New York: Appleton-Century-Crofts, 1959.

CHRISTENSEN, FRANCIS. "Problems of Defining a Mature Style." *English Journal,* vol. 57, April, 1968, pp. 572, 579.

CIARDI, JOHN. *How Does a Poem Mean?* Boston: Houghton Mifflin Co., 1959.

CUNNINGHAM, JULIA. "Dear Characters." *The Horn Book Magazine,* vol. 43, (April, 1967), pp. 233-234.

DAICHES, DAVID. "The Criticism of Fiction: Some Second Thoughts." *Literary Essays,* Oliver and Boyd, 1956. Reprinted in *An Introduction to Literary Criticism.* Edited by Marlies Danziger and W. Stacy Johnson. Lexington, Mass.: D. C. Heath & Co., 1961.

GLEASON, H. A., JR. *Linguistics and English Grammars.* New York: Holt, Rinehart & Winston, 1965.

HAYAKAWA, S. I. *Language in Thought and Action.* 2d ed. New York: Harcourt, Brace & World, 1964.

HUNT, KELLOGG W. *Grammatical Structures Written at Three Grade Levels.* NCTE Research Report No. 3. Champaign, Ill.: National Council of Teachers of English, 1965.

MICHALAK, JOANNE. "The Significance of the 'New' Grammar." In *Emerging Outlines of a New Rhetoric.* Oshkosh, Wis.: Wisconsin Council of Teachers of English, 1966.

WELLEK, RENÉ, and WARREN, AUSTIN. *Theory of Literature.* 3d ed. New York: Harcourt, Brace & World, 1956.

Selected References for Children

ALEXANDER, LLOYD. *The Book of Three.* Illustrated by Evaline Ness. New York: Holt, Rinehart & Winston, 1964.

ARMSTRONG, WILLIAM H. *Sounder.* Illustrated by James Barkley. New York: Harper & Row, 1969.

BEMELMANS, LUDWIG. *Madeline.* New York: Viking Press, 1939.

BUCKLEY, HELEN E. *Grandfather and I.* Illustrated by Paul Galdone. New York: Lothrop, Lee & Shepard Co., 1959.

CHASE, RICHARD, ed. *The Jack Tales.* Illustrated by Berkeley Williams. Boston: Houghton Mifflin Co., 1943.

———. *The Grandfather Tales.* Illustrated by Berkeley Williams. Boston: Houghton Mifflin Co., 1948.

CLAPP, PATRICIA. *Constance: A Story of Early Plymouth.* New York: Lothrop, Lee & Shepard Co., 1968.

CUNNINGHAM, JULIA. *Dorp Dead.* Illustrated by James Spanfeller. New York: Pantheon Books, 1965.

DAHL, ROALD. *Charlie and the Chocolate Factory.* Illustrated by Joseph Schindelman. New York: Alfred A. Knopf, 1964.

DEANGELI, MARGUERITE. *The Door in the Wall.* Garden City, N.Y.: Doubleday & Co., 1949.

DEJONG, MEINDERT. *Hurry Home, Candy.* Illustrated by Maurice Sendak. New York: Harper & Row, 1953.

———. *Journey from Peppermint Street.* Illustrated by Emily McCully. New York: Harper & Row, 1968.

DE REGNIERS, BEATRICE SCHENK. *May I Bring a Friend?* Illustrated by Beni Montresor. New York: Atheneum Publishers, 1964.

FRITZ, JEAN. *The Cabin Faced West.* Illustrated by Feodor Rojankovsky. New York: Coward-McCann, 1958.

JANSSON, TOVE. *Tales from Moominvalley.* New York: Henry Z. Walck, 1964.

JARRELL, RANDALL. *The Animal Family.* Illustrated by Maurice Sendak. New York: Pantheon Books, 1965.

JUSTER, NORTON. *The Phantom Tollbooth.* Illustrated by Jules Feiffer. New York: Random House, 1961.

KENDALL, CAROL. *The Gammage Cup.* Illustrated by Erik Blegvad. New York: Harcourt, Brace & World, 1959.

KIPLING, RUDYARD. *Just So Stories.* Garden City, N.Y.: Doubleday & Co., 1952.

KONIGSBURG, ELAINE L. *About the B'Nai Bagels.* New York: Atheneum Publishers, 1969.

KRUMGOLD, JOSEPH. *. . . And Now Miguel.* Illustrated by Jean Charlot. New York: Thomas Y. Crowell Co., 1953.

L'ENGLE, MADELEINE. *Meet the Austins.* New York: Vanguard Press, 1961.

———. *A Wrinkle in Time.* New York: Farrar, Straus & Giroux, 1962.

LEWIS, C. S. *The Lion, the Witch, and the Wardrobe.* Illustrated by Pauline Baynes. New York: Macmillan Co., 1950, 1961.

LIONNI, LEO. *Swimmy.* New York: Pantheon Books, 1963.

MILNE, A. A. *Winnie-the-Pooh.* Illustrated by Ernest H. Shepard. New York: E. P. Dutton & Co., 1926.

PICARD, BARBARA L. *Lost John.* Illustrated by Charles Keeping. New York: Criterion Books, 1963.

SEUSS, DR. (THEODORE SEUSS GEISEL). *One Fish, Two Fish, Red Fish, Blue Fish.* New York: Random House, 1959.

SHOTWELL, LOUISA. *Roosevelt Grady.* Illustrated by Peter Burchard. New York: World Publishing Co., 1963.

SINGER, ISAAC BASHEVIS. *Zlateh the Goat and Other Stories.* Illustrated by Maurice Sendak. New York: Harper & Row, 1966.

STEPTOE, JOHN. *Stevie.* New York: Harper & Row, 1969.

STOLZ, MARY. *Belling the Tiger.* Illustrated by Beni Montresor. New York: Harper & Row, 1961.

THURBER, JAMES. *The Thirteen Clocks*. Illustrated by Marc Simont. New York: Simon & Schuster, 1950.

WERSBA, BARBARA. *The Dream Watcher*. New York: Atheneum Publishers, 1968.

WHITE, E. B. *Charlotte's Web*. Illustrated by Garth Williams. New York: Harper & Row, 1952.

ZINDEL, PAUL. *The Pigman*. New York: Harper & Row, 1968.

chapter 5

literature study
by elementary
school children

The preceding chapters are an attempt to demonstrate that books
for children encompass literary elements similar to adult literature.
Throughout, stress has been placed on the need for parents, teachers,
and librarians both to recognize the elements of quality in literature
and to assume an attendant responsibility to share the best literature
with children. Moreover, the role of adult mentor also includes the
responsibility for developing in the child an ability to read discriminat-
ingly and a capacity to make informed judgments about his reading. In
short, it is the responsibility of the adult to guide the child toward
becoming a critical reader. This chapter, then, is directed toward a
rationale for a curriculum in literature for children of elementary school
age.

Rationale for a Literature Curriculum

A curriculum in literature has as a major objective the development
of mature critical readers. Accepting that goal establishes the need to
develop the sequential mastery of certain skills. Bruner's concept of
building complex skills on the mastery of simpler ones results in a
cyclic or spiral development.

> A curriculum should involve the mastery of skills that in turn lead
> to the mastery of still more powerful ones, the establishment of self-
> reward sequences.[1]

Bruner cites the lure of deeper understanding as both reward and in-
centive for learning. Hence, reading simple poetry makes the reading
of more complex poetry possible, and reading a poem once makes the

---

[1]Jerome S. Bruner, *Toward a Theory of Instruction* (Cambridge: The Belknap
Press of Harvard University Press, 1966), p. 35.

second reading more rewarding. Bruner's proposition for an appropriate version of any skill or knowledge reinforces the rationale for early attention to critical reading skills.

> A corollary of this conclusion (one I have urged before) is that there is an appropriate version of any skill or knowledge that may be imparted at whatever age one wishes to begin teaching—however preparatory the version may be. The choice of the earlier version is based upon what it is one is hoping to cumulate. The deepening and enrichment of this earlier understanding is again a source of reward for intellectual labors.[2]

Explicitly, then, the position taken in this book is that critical reading of literature should be taught to elementary school age children. Similarly, there are appropriate versions of critical reading skills that can be taught in an intellectually honest way to children in this age group. This position is a controversial one and must be considered in light of its criticisms and its implications for teaching perspectives.

Some of the strongest opposition to the direct teaching of literature in the elementary school came from the Anglo-American Seminar on the Teaching of English held at Dartmouth University in 1968.[3] Although the participants assumed there would and should be literature in the elementary school curriculum, they recommended an informal program at least until grades five or six.

In a more recent study of the practices of teaching literature in the elementary school, Odland reported that the study of literature is now coming into its own in American schools, in an informal but sequential pattern. She suggests that the greatest needed reform is to reintroduce *pleasure* into the English period, and that a good teacher is one who combines, wisely, a scholarly understanding of literature and an awareness of children. Her survey yielded four descriptions that characterize current approaches to teaching literature in the elementary school. These may be summarized as follows:

1. Teaching literature in a designated period of the day with the subject called *literature*. Methods are similar to those of secondary schools and college literature classes.

2. The library period and the reading guidance provided by the librarian is considered to be the literature program.

3. Teaching literature is part of a planned program for which the main objective is enjoyment of literature and continued interest

---

[2]Ibid.
[3]James R. Squire, ed., *Response to Literature* (Champaign, Ill.: National Council of Teachers of English, 1968).

in reading through developing sensitivity to literary elements as well as to content.

4. The most frequent practice is that of using literature as a secondary goal in the teaching and learning process. It may occur in reading, language arts, social studies, science, or other areas, but the objectives are only indirectly related to literature.[4]

Odland's third statement parallels the goals of a curriculum *in* literature recommended by proposals in this book.

A literature program for the elementary school structured along similar lines of the elements of literature was proposed earlier by Huck.[5] She stated that children need to be guided in the identification and analysis of the basic elements of literature which she lists as characterization, diction, tone, theme, point of view, style, genre, and structure. Teaching literature as a planned program for which the main objective is enjoyment of literature is a worthy and realistic goal. Such a program should also stress continued interest in reading by developing a sensitivity to literary elements and content. The ordering and design of the content must be done with knowledge about the children who will participate, as well as knowledge about literature. There are numerous prototypes in circulation illustrating the designs of such a literature curriculum; some were described in Chapter 1, and three designs are described here.

Strong support exists for assigning poetry a central role in an elementary school literature curriculum since it builds upon the natural rhythm of children, illustrates the rhythm of language, and helps to illustrate the ways one can play with language. Northrop Frye says elementary school children should start at the center with poetry, move through literary prose next before dealing with languages of the businesses, professions, and ordinary life.[6] Poetry as the central and unifying component of a curriculum in literature is a valid approach. Inasmuch as the focus for this textbook was narrative fiction, and poetry is treated in another book in this series, it was not examined here. Poetry cannot be ignored, however, in a proposal for a literature curriculum, nor can any other literary form. In order to achieve balance in a literature curriculum, some exposure must be given to all forms.

Haley supports the approach to literature through poetry that stresses the rock and swing and the pull and push of words. He would

---

[4]Norine Odland, *Teaching Literature in the Elementary School* (Champaign, Ill.: National Council of Teachers of English, 1969), pp. 44-52.

[5]Charlotte S. Huck, "Children's Literature in an Institute for Elementary Teachers," *Source Book on English Institutes for Elementary Teachers* (Champaign, Ill.: National Council of Teachers of English, 1965), pp. 11-18.

[6]Northrop Frye, *The Educated Imagination* (Bloomington, Ind.: Indiana University Press, 1964), p. 122.

also play word games and have children do anything that makes language appear to them as rich and slippery, rewarding and amazing, and just plain fun.

> When they read a story that begins "once upon a time" and ends "they lived happily ever after," they could ask "Why?" That set of formulas makes a fairy tale frame. Why a fairy tale frame? What should we expect in between? Magic. Certain kinds of terror. Enchantments. Marvelous rescues. Charms. Good fairies and bad. But what if the bad ones win? What if the happy ending really isn't happy? What is the writer doing? And so they grow to ask the kind of questions that cause them to know what irony is, and tone of voice, and what kind of expectations to have, and when to be surprised and when to sense that the usual form of things is being worked out according to a schedule.[7]

A comprehensive approach to a literature curriculum was developed by teachers in Wisconsin for kindergarten through grade twelve.[8] It included poetry, folk and fairy tales, Bible stories, realistic and fanciful novels, hero tales, and biographies. The Wisconsin literature curriculum is based upon the concept that growth in literary sensitivity, taste, and discrimination is sequential and cumulative. Their stated belief that every step in the process of learning to enjoy and appreciate literature depends upon previous experiences and learnings prompted them to publish the K-12 curriculum as an integral unit. Success of instruction in the program is measured by students' ability to deal with literature at various levels of interpretation, using many skills of analysis. Despite a variety of designs for the literature curriculum, there exists strong opposition to a sequential program focused upon the content and form of the literature itself.

The Issue of Teaching Literary Criticism

Britton is representative of those who contend that literary criticism should not be taught in the elementary school. He insists that children and teachers should talk about the people and events of literature, but not about the forms, conventions, devices, and techniques. With reference to formal analysis, Britton chides:

> To have children take over from their teachers an analysis of a work of literature which their teachers in turn have taken over from the

---

[7]Leroy D. Haley, "A Dramatistic Approach to Composition," *Emerging Outlines of a New Rhetoric* (Oshkosh, Wis.: Wisconsin Council of Teachers of English, 1966), pp. 14-15.

[8]Wisconsin English Language Arts Curriculum Project, *Teaching Literature in Wisconsin* (Madison: State of Wisconsin Department of Public Instruction, 1965).

critics or their English professors—this is not a shortcut to literary sophistication; it is a short circuit that destroys the whole system.[9]

Such an exercise, Britton would surely admit, does not meet Bruner's (or anyone's) criteria of appropriateness and intellectual honesty at *any* academic level. Others at the Dartmouth Seminars reinforced Britton's admonition by emphasizing that formal study of literary criticism, literary history, and critical theory is inappropriate at the elementary school level. Harding, for example, insisted that

> The dryness of schematic analysis of imagery, symbols, myth, structural relations et. al, should be avoided passionately at school and often at college. *It is literature, not literary criticism, which is the subject.*[10]

The arid analysis and sterile formalism described by Britton and Harding should be intently eschewed. Undoubtedly, they refer to the frequently mismanaged literature program of some high schools. No one would seriously condone a downward extension and repetition of such misplaced emphasis in a literature curriculum for younger pupils.

The point underscored here is that the issue seems to be drawn in terms of an unreal contrast. Do either complete freedom of choice and spontaneous curiosity in literature or a highly structured program of formalistic critical analysis constitute the only available options? Gardner Murphy aptly takes exception to such polarized veiw of guiding learning:

> Is there necessarily an intrinsic conflict between encouraging the spontaneous curiosity, interest, enthusiasm, and love of knowing in the child, and also guiding him, helping him to focus, organize, master thoroughly and proudly the skills and insights involved in the areas of his most eager knowing?[11]

Those concerned with children's reading habits advocate, almost universally, that children read widely and frequently. There seems to be a consensus, also, that children learn to discriminate between good and poor literature. Until such attitudes of appreciation and skills of discrimination are shown to be acquired with the rites of passage to adolescence, contention as to how they are best developed is a valid educational issue.

---

[9]James Britton, "Response to Literature," *Response to Literature,* ed. James R. Squire (Champaign, Ill.: National Council of Teachers of English, 1968), p. 6.
[10]D. W. Harding, "Response to Literature: The Report of the Study Group," *Response to Literature,* ed. James R. Squire (Champaign, Ill.: National Council of Teachers of English, 1968), p. 26, (author's italics).
[11]Gardner Murphy, *Freeing Intelligence through Teaching* (New York: Harper & Row, Publishers, 1961), pp. 26-27.

Even very young children have a great many books, both good and poor, from which to choose. As their functional ability to read improves, the number of books available to them increases almost exponentially. The better children can read literally, the greater the need to discriminate among their choices.

Adults, particularly parents, teachers, and librarians, serve in some advisory capacity in helping children select their literature throughout the elementary school years. Their advisory role evolves from one of sole decision on books for the child, to mutual choice and, eventually, to rather complete independence of the child in the book selection process. Whether decisions are made by an adult or a child, selection criteria are based on the elements of literature treated in this book, regardless of labels. Awareness of the process in which one engages should have a propitious effect upon the activity. Related to a curriculum *in* literature, learning the skills required to make adequate choices is a sequential process moving from the simple to the complex. In Bruner's terms, the choice of the earlier skills depends upon what one is aiming to accrue. If the goal is to help children become independent discriminating readers, then there are appropriate preliminary skills they should learn either in school, at a library, or in the home. The controversial issue deals more appropriately with *how* children shall be taught the skills related to literature; the choice is *not* between formalized instruction in literary criticism and unguided spontaneous enthusiasm.

Approaches to Critical Reading

The question as to how the development of discriminating readers can be approached with elementary school children is incisively put by Loban:

> Because literature has both a concern with the humanistic worth of its content and the aesthetic beauty of its form, its two aspects can seldom be separated. A presentation of human values devoid of artistic form is no more memorable than a guidance pamphlet on being a good brother; beautiful literary form without meaningful content is interesting, but not as enchanting as music.

Insisting on the need for considering both content and form, Loban proposes a balanced but nonformalistic approach:

> In seeking a balance for a literature program, then, teachers will wish to include various kinds of content relevant to the world of the child and his growth; they will also wish to make use of the full range of artistry children may encounter in literature—form, irony, symbolism, and all the language of metaphor on which literature depends. This range of content and artistry can be included without

formal study or examination. Such intellectual instruction in literary
form does not belong in the elementary school.[12]

This proposal stresses recognition of the humanistic values, as well
as the aesthetic qualities of literature cited by Rosenheim in the first
chapter of this book. Moreover, it reiterates earlier cautions that direct
intellectual instruction in literary form is inappropriate for elementary
schools. How, then, the question arises, is use made of the full range
of literary artistry encountered in developing appreciation and skill?
What processes may teachers, librarians, and parents employ for stimulating the growth of discriminating young readers?

A promising avenue is suggested by the Commission on English.

> In the elementary grades or later, with very unsophisticated students,
> the teacher may do nothing but read good works aloud, interpreting
> them through intonation, emphasis, pacing, and a multitude of hardly
> noticeable indications of thought and feeling. Usually, however, the
> teacher as critic asks questions, primarily because criticism is a pro-
> cess of asking questions and attempting to answer them. Question
> asking is the process the students must learn, becoming critics them-
> selves as they become increasingly adept at asking their own ques-
> tions and at seeking and testing their answers. And gradually they
> must learn also to ask what kinds of questions they are asking, what
> kinds of answers they are seeking.[13]

The kernel of this proposal lies in the matter of questioning. Seemingly
a Socratic approach, nonetheless, questioning is natural to children, and
it functions to provide them with information and order from their
experiences. Even the advocates of a laissez-faire approach to literature
for children acknowledge that discussion and exchange about experiences
with books is beneficial. The Commission statement indicates that children should become adept at asking questions, and it implies that teachers serve as modelers of questions. More importantly, it points out that,
gradually, children must reflect upon the kinds of questions they are
asking and the answers they are seeking. In other words, reflection on,
and interpretation of, one's experiences is what education is all about.
Finally, there is an appropriate version and an intellectually honest form
of developing skills of questioning and of evaluating experiences with
literature for elementary school children.

The major approach to critical reading, then, is through perfecting
the question-asking skills of both the adult mentor and the child reader.

---

[12]Walter Loban, "Balancing the Literature Program," *Elementary English*, vol.
43, (November, 1966), Champaign, Ill.: National Council of Teachers of English,
p. 747.
[13]*Freedom and Discipline in English: Report of the Commission on English*
(New York: The College Entrance Examination Board, 1965), p. 55. Copyright ©
1965 by The College Entrance Examination Board and reprinted with their permission.

The adult who engages in dialogue with children as they interpret their literature not only serves as a model, but stimulates and elicits the kinds of questioning behavior he values. One of the many findings from the Ohio State University Critical Reading Project was that teachers elicited the level of thinking they asked for in their questions.[14] Teachers who continued to ask literal questions obtained factual responses from students, but those who requested evaluative and analytical responses obtained them frequently. There was a relationship between the kinds of questions teachers asked and the level of critical responses given by the pupils.

In order for adults working with children and literature to recognize the level and direction of their own and children's questions, it is advisable that they view questions in relation to a total framework for a literature curriculum. Several frameworks are available, and three will be described here. First, materials developed during the Critical Reading Project provide a categorization of critical reading skills and the levels of questions. The list of skills for the critical reading of all types of materials includes informational, persuasive, and literary. Specifically related to literature are numerous skills: recognizing various genre of fiction; distinguishing among forms; identifying and evaluating characterization, plot structure, setting, and theme; and identifying and evaluating the author's use of language, his mood of writing, and his point of view.[15]

In addition to the list of skills, an instrument for observing the teaching of critical reading was developed, one that served to categorize the type of question asked and the level of thinking elicited by it. Teachers who asked more clarifying, analyzing, and evaluating types of questions obtained higher-level thinking responses from their students than did those who asked factual, interpreting, and applying types of questions.[16] Examining illustrative questions provided by the authors can alert one to ascertain the level of his own or his students' questions.

Huck and Kuhn refined and extended the categorization of literary understandings and skills into a taxonomy.[17] Their comprehensive taxonomy includes numerous specific skills under headings such as understands types of literature, understands components of fiction, understands components of poetry, evaluates literature, and applies knowledge

---

[14]Willavene Wolf, Charlotte S. Huck, and Martha L. King, with Bernice Ellinger Cullinan, *Critical Reading Ability of Elementary School Children*, United States Office of Education Project No. 5-1040, Contract No. OE-4-10-187, (June, 1967), p. 98.

[15]Ibid., pp. 20-22.

[16]Ibid., p. 95.

[17]Charlotte S. Huck and Doris Young Kuhn, *Children's Literature in the Elementary School*, 2d ed. (New York: Holt, Rinehart & Winston, 1968), pp. 688-691.

of literary criticism. Using this taxonomy as a checklist, a teacher, parent, or librarian could quickly identify the type of question he or a child was asking about a selection and could be cognizant of other areas in which he might question.

Purves made a significant contribution toward understanding interaction with literature through an empirical investigation of teachers', students', and critics' written responses to a literary work.[18] After listing all the responses made, he grouped them according to similarities and suggested that all responses to literature could be categorized according to four major conceptualizations. The four general relationships that emerged from his study were: (a) the direct interaction of the responder and the literary work, including much of what hampers that interaction; (b) the responder viewing the work and its author as objects; (c) the responder relating the universe portrayed in the literary work to the universe as he conceives it to be; and (d) the responder judging the literary work in relation to the artist, the universe, and himself. Purves assigned labels to the conceptualizations, corresponding to the order listed above, as (a) engagement-involvement, (b) perception, (c) interpretations, and (d) evaluation.

He defines *engagement-involvement* as the ways by which a reader indicates his surrender to a literary work; it can be highly subjective and unassailable by logic or persuasion. *Perception* encompasses the ways in which a person looks at a literary work as an object in an analytic, synthetic, or classificatory way and deals with it in isolation or as a historical fact. *Interpretation* incorporates the ways a reader draws from the literary work connections to his own world. It includes a reader finding meaning in the work, drawing generalizations, and finding analogies in his own world. *Evaluation* encompasses all statements about the reader's reasons for thinking a work is good or bad. His judgment may be derived from either personal or objective criteria, and it roughly parallels the elements cited in the other categories, for his evaluation is based on his engagement-involvement, his perception, or his interpretation. Purves proposes the literary work and the individual who responds to it as the foci for any statements that can be made about a work, and these two theoretical foci as educational foci. More than anything else, Purves sees the elements and categories providing a way of thinking about the literature curriculum and the teaching process.[19] Undoubtedly, it provides a suitable frame of reference

---

[18]Alan C. Purves, with Victoria Rippere. *Elements of Writing about a Literary Work: A Study of Response to Literature* (Champaign, Ill.: National Council of Teachers of English, 1968), p. 6. Copyright © by Alan C. Purves. Reprinted with permission of National Council of Teachers of English.

[19]Ibid., pp. 64-65.

for viewing questions and statements about literature. A question or statement indicating engagement-involvement would not be acknowledged in the same way as a statement or question of perception. Furthermore, the bases, implications, and relationships of questions and statements can be made explicit so that responders become aware of what they are doing. As they become more self-conscious, they become more self-reliant. Purves asks the rhetorical question, does this self-consciousness inhibit enjoyment of literature? Among other things, he says

> . . . omnivorous reading without any thought is of equally tarnished value. The unthinking absorption of books is peripherally educational in the same way as is intricate analysis pursued for its own sake. There is, however, a balance, and this balance would seem to be the aspiration of education in literature.[20]

This statement reiterates previous ones requesting balance in the literature curriculum; the polemists dare not prevail that either unthinking absorption or intricate analysis are the only alternatives. A final statement by Purves reinforces his plea for tentativeness in teaching literature. He believes that the comprehensiveness of the elements and categories identified illustrate to any teacher that the choices he makes in approaching a literature curriculum must be recognized as merely choices. Since none could approach instruction in literature with more than a limited number of possibilities, he must recognize the tentativeness of his approach. Purves hopes the recognition that any one approach to literature cannot be all-encompassing will encourage teachers to be flexible in their treatment of literary study.[21]

In essence, the direction of literary instruction with elementary school age children in schools, homes, or libraries is toward the development of self-conscious awareness of one's engagement with literature and the expression of that engagement. Ideally, the process of examining one's engagement leads to an awareness of the literary forces that act on the individual, of his values, and of his own sensibility—without losing the initial spark of the engagement. Education comes through the discussion of the bases for evaluation, not the conclusions.

The approach to literary criticism with children is a part of one's total approach to the education of children. For those people who assume the role of dispenser of information and ultimate authority source for children, a warning that literature must not be shared in that way will have little effect on their behavior. For those teachers, parents, and librarians who respect the intelligence of children, who provide opportunities for children to learn, who follow cues from the

---

[20]Ibid., p. 63.
[21]Ibid., p. 65.

child about what he wants to know, and who engage in dialogues with children, respecting their ideas, there is no need for warnings. Teachers, parents, and librarians in the latter group will help children obtain meaning from their literature in as many ways as the child can absorb. They will explore literature with children and help them examine the processes in which they engage, but they will not conduct quiz sessions, such as what is the plot, who were the main characters, and what is the theme? The true critic will recognize the validity of emotional responses to literature; he will acknowledge engagement-involvement responses as appropriate and acceptable. He will also recognize when it is appropriate to encourage a child to intellectualize about an aesthetic experience. Even as he encourages a child to intellectualize about the aesthetic experience, he will evaluate the purpose for which it is done. There can be no other valid purpose than to increase a child's appreciation, to heighten the level of his understanding, and to provide him with increasingly successful experiences in making wise choices for his independent reading. In this way, he becomes a critic of his own literature.

Summary

Teachers, parents, and librarians who recognize elements of quality in literature have an attendant responsibility to develop in children the ability to discriminate quality and to make informed judgments about their own reading. Accepting the goal of developing critical readers obligates adults to identify sequential mastery of specific skills leading to that goal. There are appropriate versions of the skills and knowledge requisite to critical reading of literature that may be imparted to elementary school age children. Current practices most frequently used in teaching literature to elementary school children are those in which literature contributes to understanding in other areas of the curriculum but which are seldom related directly to literature itself. A realistic and worthwhile framework for a literature curriculum is a planned program in which the main objective is enjoyment of literature, with continued interest in reading developing through sensitivity to literary elements and content.

Arid analyses and formalistic literary criticism are inappropriate in the elementary school, but the choice is not one of extremes. The controversy over literary criticism in the elementary school deals more precisely with the *way* children are taught to make critical judgments about their literature. Stimulating critical questions and eliciting higher level thinking skills are suitable for the process of developing mature critical readers.

Activities for Further Study

1. Survey the practices of elementary teachers regarding the use of literature in the elementary school curriculum. Ask how many use literature in other subject areas and how many use it to develop understandings related to literature itself.

2. Develop a questionnaire of terms dealing with literary criticism. Administer it to the teachers in your school. From the results, summarize areas of competence and need.

3. Use Purves' conceptualizations of engagement-involvement, perception, interpretation, and evaluation to examine the responses made by children after hearing a literary selection read aloud. Although James Squire stated that the written responses may not be the same as other responses to literature, see if stated ones can be categorized according to Purves' system.

4. Tape record a discussion of a literary selection that you have read to a group of children. Categorize your questions and children's questions according to the Wolf, Huck, King category system of gathering specific facts, clarifying, interpreting or inferring from facts, analyzing, applying, summarizing, and evaluating.

5. Develop an interview guide dealing with the question of teaching literary criticism in the elementary school. Start with questions inferring formalistic analysis procedures and gradually move to questions inferring deeper meaning from literature than surface level reading. See how many teachers are opposed to the original position but accept the latter position of reading for deeper meanings.

6. Obtain several literature curriculum guides and examine them for the following points:
    (a) stated objectives
    (b) content to be taught
    (c) skills to be developed
    (d) materials to be used
    (e) activities suggested

7. Several publishers have developed literature readers. Examine the sets produced to see what kind of balance is incorporated in the selections, what skills and concepts are suggested in the teachers' manuals, and what related activities and readings they suggest.

Selected References

BRITTON, JAMES. "Response to Literature," in *Response to Literature*. Edited by James Squire. Champaign, Ill.: National Council of Teachers of English, 1968.

BRUNER, JEROME S. *Toward a Theory of Instruction*. Cambridge: The Belknap Press of the Harvard University Press, 1966.

Commission on English. *Freedom and Discipline in English: Report of the Commission on English*. New York: The College Entrance Examination Board, 1965.

FRYE, NORTHROP. *The Educated Imagination*. Bloomington, Ind.: Indiana University Press, 1964.

HALEY, LEROY D. "A Dramatistic Approach to Composition," in *Emerging Outlines of a New Rhetoric*. Oshkosh, Wis.: Wisconsin Council of Teachers of English, 1966.

HARDING, D. W. "Response to Literature: The Report of the Study Group," in *Response to Literature*. Edited by James Squire. Champaign, Ill.: National Council of Teachers of English, 1968.

HUCK, CHARLOTTE S. "Children's Literature in an Institute for Elementary Teachers," in *Source Book on English Institutes for Elementary Teachers*. Champaign, Ill.: National Council of Teachers of English, 1965.

HUCK, CHARLOTTE S., and KUHN, DORIS YOUNG. *Children's Literature in the Elementary School*. New York: Holt, Rinehart & Winston, 1968.

LOBAN, WALTER. "Balancing the Literature Program," *Elementary English*, vol. 43, November, 1966. National Council of Teachers of English.

MURPHY, GARDNER. *Freeing Intelligence through Teaching*. New York: Harper & Row, Publishers, 1961.

ODLAND, NORINE. *Teaching Literature in the Elementary School*. Champaign, Ill.: National Council of Teachers of English, 1969.

PURVES, ALAN C., with RIPPERE, VICTORIA. *Elements of Writing about a Literary Work: A Study of Response to Literature*. Champaign, Ill.: National Council of Teachers of English, 1968.

SQUIRE, JAMES R., ed. *Response to Literature*. Champaign, Ill.: National Council of Teachers of English, 1968.

Wisconsin English Language Arts Curriculum Project, *Teaching Literature in Wisconsin*. Madison: State of Wisconsin Department of Public Instruction, 1965.

WOLF, WILLAVENE; HUCK, CHARLOTTE S.; and KING, MARTHA L.; with CULLINAN, BERNICE ELLINGER. *Critical Reading Ability of Elementary School Children*. United States Office of Education Project No. 5-1040, Contract No. OE-4-10-187, June, 1967.

annotated bibliography
on literary criticism
and children's literature

ALTICK, RICHARD D. *Preface to Critical Reading.* 4th ed. New York: Holt, Rinehart & Winston, 1962.
Basic instruction with many examples in reading fiction and nonfiction critically. The relationship between critical reading and effective writing is specifically defined and analyzed.

ARBUTHNOT, MAY HILL. *Children and Books.* 3d ed. Glenview, Ill.: Scott, Foresman & Co., 1964.
A basic text in the field of children's literature. Theories of the development of folk literature and mythology are provided.

AUERBACH, ERICH. *Mimesis: The Representation of Reality in Western Literature.* Garden City, N.Y.: Doubleday Anchor Books, 1957.
A study of the ways Western writers, from Homer to Virginia Woolf, have used language and rhetoric to project their versions of reality. The first chapter presents the two main styles that influence the representation of reality in European literature.

BROOKS, CLEANTH, and WARREN, ROBERT PENN. *Understanding Fiction.* 2d ed. New York: Appleton-Century-Crofts, 1959.
A collection of literary works with suggested guides for intensive reading. The authors believe that before extensive reading can be profitable, some practice in intensive reading is needed. An appendix of technical problems and principles in the composition of fiction summarizing concepts developed fully in the text is included.

DAICHES, DAVID. *Critical Approaches to Literature.* Englewood Cliffs, N. J.: Prentice-Hall, 1956.
A book that intends to reveal the nature both of literature and of criticism by presenting some of the ways literature has been discussed. It is divided into three sections: critical discussions of the nature, use, and value of imaginative literature; practical criticism and evaluation of specific literary works; and the relationship between literary criticism and other disciplines.

FRYE, NORTHROP. *Anatomy of Criticism.* Princeton, N. J.: Princeton University Press, 1957.

The author wishes to acknowledge the assistance of Barbara Kleger in the preparation of this bibliography.

An attempt, according to Frye, to demonstrate the possibility of a synoptic view of the scope, theory, principles, and techniques of literary criticism. A presentation of theories, modes, symbols, myths, and genres.

GEORGIOU, CONSTANTINE. *Children and Their Literature.* Englewood Cliffs, N. J.: Prentice-Hall, 1969.
A carefully illustrated textbook that demonstrates the comprehensive nature of the field of children's literature. Criteria for evaluating each of the divisions of literature are given.

HAZARD, PAUL. *Books, Children and Men.* Boston: The Horn Book, 1960.
A classic statement on the need to maintain the integrity of childhood and the literature provided for children. A historical perspective on the injustices done to children through their literature and, conversely, a citation of much that is worthwhile.

HUCK, CHARLOTTE, and KUHN, DORIS YOUNG. *Children's Literature in the Elementary School.* 2d ed. New York: Holt, Rinehart & Winston, 1968.
Classic textbook in children's literature which covers content, criteria, and use of children's literature in elementary school curricula. Comprehensive coverage of high quality literature within each of the divisions of literature, criteria for selecting books of quality, and illustrations of teaching literary criticism in the elementary school are given.

JAMES, HENRY. *The Art of the Novel. Critical Prefaces.* New York: Charles Scribner's Sons, 1934.
James' prefaces in which he criticizes specifically his own work and writes both an essay in general criticism and a reference book on the technical aspects of the art of fiction.

LEWIS, C. S. *An Experiment in Criticism.* Cambridge: Cambridge University Press, 1961.
An essay which attempts to define a good book by the way in which it is read, and to understand what good reading is.

LUBBOCK, PERCY. *The Art of Fiction.* New York: Charles Scribner's Sons, 1955.
A study of the techniques of writers in presenting their stories, with the main interest on methods of making novels.

MEIGS, CORNELIA; EATON, ANNE THAXTER; NESBITT, ELIZABETH; and VIGUERS, RUTH HILL. *A Critical History of Children's Literature.* New York: Macmillan Co., 1953.
Describes the development of children's literature and the much later development of literary criticism in this field. The chronology provides a historical perspective of the influences shaping children's literature.

OGDEN, C. K., and RICHARDS, I. A. *The Meaning of Meaning.* 3d ed. New York: Harcourt, Brace & World, 1930.
A thorough examination of the use of signs for symbolic purposes and for emotive purposes aimed at increasing the precision with which language is used.

POTTS, L. J., ed. and trans. *Aristotle on the Art of Fiction.* Cambridge: Cambridge University Press, 1968.
A translation of Aristotle's theory of poetry, the *Poetics*, with an introductory essay and explanatory notes.

RICHARDS, I. A. *Practical Criticism: A Study of Literary Judgment.* New York: Harcourt, Brace & World, 1929.
A classic forerunner to Purves' attempt to categorize responses to literature. Richards includes poems, reactions to the poems, with his analysis

of the poetry and the responses. He attempts to develop new methods for developing discrimination and power to understand what is read and heard.

ROSENHEIM, EDWARD W., JR. *What Happens in Literature.* Chicago: Phoenix Books, The University of Chicago Press, 1960.
A book which tries to help the reader to acquire habits and information that will lead to a rewarding experience with many literary works, each seen as a unique encounter.

SCHOLES, ROBERT, and KELLOGG, ROBERT. *The Nature of Narrative.* Oxford: Clarendon Press, 1966.
A historical and analytical study that considers the elements common to all narrative forms, from myth and folktale to novels. Relates the historical development of character, plot, meaning, and point of view in narrative.

SMITH, LILLIAN H. *The Unreluctant Years.* Chicago: American Library Association, 1953.
A book that attempts to reveal the literary merits of children's books and the standards of good writing by which they can be judged. Individual chapters deal with different types of literature, such as fairy tale, folktale, and realistic and historical fiction.

TOLKIEN, J. R. R. *Tree and Leaf.* Boston: Houghton Mifflin Co., 1965.
A book consisting of an essay on fairy stories and a short story. In the essay, Tolkien discusses the particular values of the fairy story and how it differs from other forms of fantasy.

TOWNSEND, JOHN ROWE. *Written for Children.* New York: Lothrop, Lee & Shepard Co., 1965.
A historical account of English prose fiction for children, enriched with examples. This source is basic to an understanding of American children's literature.

WELLEK, RENÉ and WARREN, AUSTIN. *Theory of Literature.* 3d ed. New York: Harcourt, Brace & World, 1956.
A book that tries to unite the theory and criticism of literature with literary scholarship and history. It examines the nature, content, form, and function of literature.

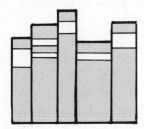

index